C000088529

Coastal Guides FROM THE **AIR**

The Normandy Coast from the Air

Cap de la Hague to Cap Fréhel

Published by Adlard Coles Nautical
An imprint of A & C Black Publishers Ltd
36 Soho Square, London W1D 3QY
www.adlardcoles.com

First UK edition published in 2010.

© Originally published in French as *Le Littoral Du Cap de la Hague au Cap Fréhel* by GALLIMARD LOISIRS, 2006

Original text by Jean-Louis Guéry
Photos by Éric Guillemot
Cartography by Philippe Doussinet & Edigraphie
Illustrations by Gilbert Houbre, Pascal Robin, François Desbordes, Jean Chevallier, Dominique Mansion, Claire Felloni

ISBN 978-1-4081-1276-2

All rights reserved. No part of this publication may be reproduced in any form or by any means - graphic, electronic or mechanical, including photocopying, recording, taping or information storage and retrieval systems - without the prior permission in writing of the publishers.

The right of the author to be identified as the author of this work has been asserted by him in accordance with the Copyright, Designs and Patents Act, 1988.

A CIP catalogue record for this book is available from the British Library.

This book is produced using paper that is made from wood grown in managed, sustainable forests. It is natural, renewable and recyclable. The logging and manufacturing processes conform to the environmental regulations of the country of origin.

Typeset in 8.5pt on 9.25 pt Frutiger Light
Printed and bound in China by Leo Paper Products

Note: *While all reasonable care has been taken in the publication of this book, the publisher takes no responsibility for the use of the methods or products described in the book.*

The charts in this publication are not suitable for navigation. Refer to Admiralty or Imray charts of the area.

Coastal Guides FROM THE AIR

The Normandy Coast from the Air
Cap de la Hague to Cap Fréhel

Photos by Éric Guillemot,
Original text by Jean-Louis Guéry
Edited by Jane Cumberlidge

ADLARD COLES NAUTICAL
LONDON

CONTENTS

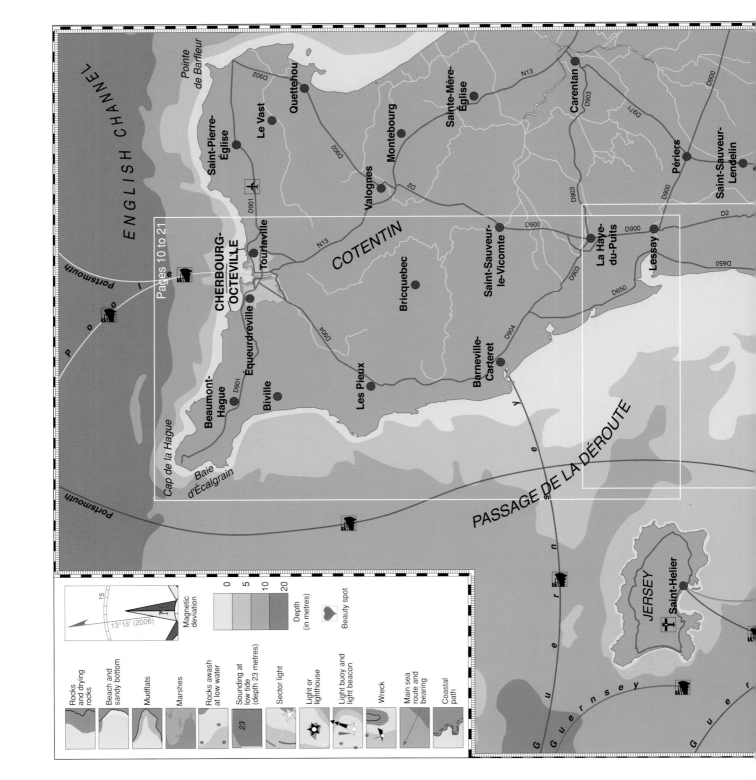

ENGLISH CHANNEL

Portsmouth

Portsmouth

Pages 10 to 21

Pointe de Barfleur

Quettehou

Le Vast

Saint-Pierre-Église

D902

D902

D901

Tourlaville

CHERBOURG-OCTEVILLE

Équeurdreville

Beaumont-Hague

Biville

D901

Cap de la Hague

Baie d'Écalgrain

Montebourg

Sainte-Mère-Église

Valognes

D2

N13

COTENTIN

Bricquebec

Les Pieux

D904

Saint-Sauveur-le-Vicomte

Barneville-Carteret

D904

N13

D900

D903

Carentan

N13

D903

D971

Périers

D900

D900

Saint-Sauveur-Lendelin

D2

La Haye-du-Puits

D903

D650

Lessay

D900

D650

D2

D660

PASSAGE DE LA DÉROUTE

Guernsey

Guernsey

Guer

JERSEY

Saint-Helier

Magnetic deviation

15

13°16' (2006)

0
5
10
20

Depth (in metres)

Beauty spot

Rocks and drying rocks

Beach and sandy bottom

Mudflats

Marshes

Rocks awash at low water

Sounding at low tide (depth 23 metres)

23

Sector light

Light or lighthouse

Light buoy and light beacon

Wreck

Main sea route and bearing

Coastal path

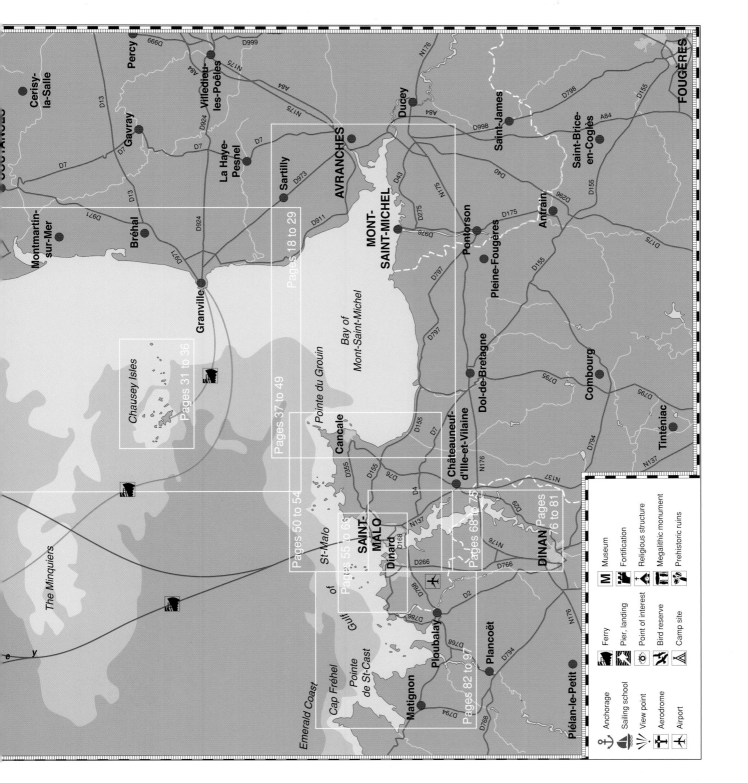

West Cotentin and the Chausey Archipelago

From Cap de la Hague to Granville, the west coast of the Cotentin peninsula has a unique and special character. A variety of landscapes stretch over nearly 100 kilometres and each expanse is more compelling than the last. To the north, precipitous headlands jut out into fast tidal waters and notorious passages such as the turbulent Alderney Race and the rocky Passage de la Déroute. Further south, the coastal currents have carved dramatic sandy inlets where the dunes, rivers and tides are locked in a continuing struggle against each other. This spectacular coastline of wild estuaries and havens has many attractions, from the snug coastal harbours, to the rich, rare and varied flora and fauna inland. Ten miles out to sea, surrounded by powerful tidal streams, the Chausey Islands form yet another world. At low tide the Chausey plateau is a labyrinth of islands, reefs and drying banks, but at high water only Grande-Île and a handful of islets and heads remain visible. Grande-Île has a restaurant, a bar and a few small fishermen's cottages, and the islanders are fiercely independent.

1. A scattering of islets at the heart of Chausey; in less than an hour they'll be submerged by the tide.
2. Granville's historic quarter.

1

2

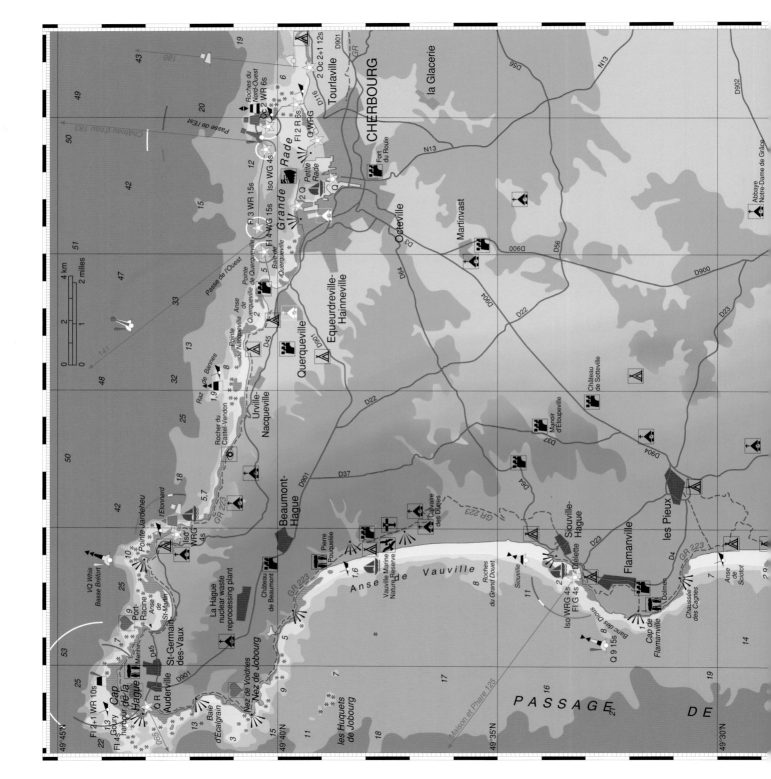

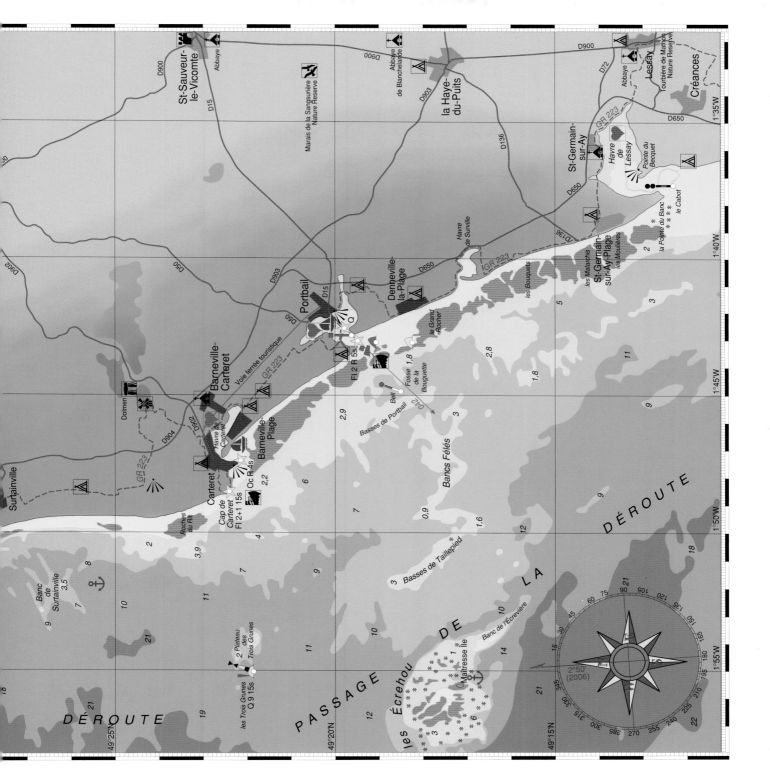

St-Sauveur-le-Vicomte

Abbaye

D900

D15

D900

Abbaye de Blanchelande

D900

Marais de la Sangsurière Nature Reserve

D903

la Haye-du-Puits

D136

Lessay

Abbaye

D72

Tourbière de Mathon Nature Reserve

Créances

D650

St-Germain-sur-Ay

GR 223

Havre de Lessay

Pointe du Bécquet

la Pointe du Banc

le Cabot

D650

2

D136

Havre de Surville

GR 223

St-Germain-sur-Ay-Plage

les Moulières

2

les Malardis

les Bouquets

3

5

2,8

1,8

11

Denneville-la-Plage

D650

Portbail

D15

Voie ferrée touristique

GR 223

Q

Fl 2 R 5s

le Grand Rocher

Fosse 1,8 de la Bouguette

3

Bell

Basses de Portbail

2,9

6

3

Bancs Félés

9

9

Barneville-Carteret

Dolmen

D902

D904

Havre de Carteret

GR 223

Barneville-Plage

Oc R 4s

2,2

7

0,9

1,6

12

DÉROUTE

Surtainville

Carteret

Roches du Rit

Cap de Carteret Fl 2+1 15s

4

3,9

2

7

9

3

Basses de Taillepied

LA

18

Banc de Surtainville

3,5

8

7

9

10

21

11

7

9

10

Banc de l'Écrevière

14

105

90

75

60

45

30

15

0

345

330

120

135

150

165

180

195

210

225

240

255

270

285

300

315

2°50' (2006)

18

21

DÉROUTE

19

les Trois Grunes Q 9 15s

2 Plateau des Trois Grunes

11

12

10

Maîtresse Île

1

21

22

PASSAGE

DE

les Écrehou

6

3

49°25'N

49°20'N

49°15'N

90

D902

D50

D903

D50

D50

1°35'W

1°40'W

1°45'W

1°50'W

1°55'W

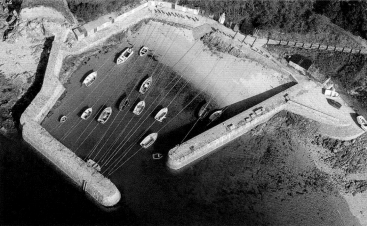

Saint-Germain-des-Vaux   Auderville

Anse de Saint-Martin   Pointe du Nez

La Hague lighthouse   Cap de la Hague
Goury

Baie d'Écalgrain

Nez de Voidries   Nez de Jobourg   Anse de Pivette

Cap de la Hague

The cliffs and Nez de Joburg
Rising to 127m above Sennival cove, the Jobourg headland is much steeper than Nez de Voidries, though not nearly as high. The caves at the foot of Voidries are completely inaccessible, even to experienced climbers.

Cap de la Hague is one of the great headlands along this coast. This harsh, austere promontory is swept by the formidable Alderney Race, whose moods and dangers are well known to mariners. Here, the tidal streams between Alderney and the headland are amongst the fastest in the world, reaching nearly 10 knots at top spring tides. Then the race becomes a raging torrent and, if the wind is against the tide, a seething cauldron with chaotic breakers which even larger ships avoid. Needless to say, this formidable sea area is home to many terrifying legends.

The Cotentin hinterland is charming: a countryside of beautiful valleys and small villages where traditional patterns of life are well preserved. At Omonville-la-Petite you can admire the *bijudes*, ancient stone houses with thatched roofs.

Jacques Prévert, a French poet and screenwriter, died in the hamlet of Val having retired to this sleepy corner of Normandy. His body rests in the Omonville sailors' cemetery.

An exploration of this region can begin at Saint-Martin, where France's smallest harbour is part of the commune of Saint-Germain-des-Vaux. Port-Racine is so tiny that its jetties seem to be built for model boats. The pool hardly looks wide enough to take even a handful of dinghies. Port-Racine is named after its founder, the pirate François-Médard Racine, who built this minuscule haven in the 19th century

to shelter small fishing craft from La Hague that worked the Alderney Race for mackerel and bass. Returning to Port-Racine, these boats had to wait for enough rise of tide in their small but cosy home port, whose entrance gap is barely three metres between the breakwaters. Sailors say that a single wave is enough to fill it!

Nearby Port Goury isn't very large either, tucked in behind the lighthouse at Cap de la Hague. The original octagonal lifeboat station at Goury is well known for many brave and difficult rescues, but looks an insignificant place given the dangers that surround it.

Past Auderville, the coast path falls towards Écalgrain Bay, from where you can see the austere silhouettes of Nez de Voidries and

Goury　La Hague lighthouse　　Cap de la Hague

Hâvre de Bombec

Port-Racine　　Les Herbeuses

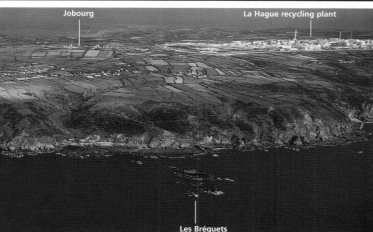

Jobourg　　La Hague recycling plant

Les Bréquets

Nez de Jobourg to the south, linked by the small cove at Sennival where the water is strikingly clear. The sheer cliff towers more than 100 metres above the sea and it is dangerous for walkers to leave the marked trail – accidents happen here every year.

The radar towers of the Regional Search and Rescue Centre are located at Nez de Jobourg. This important control centre monitors and records the movements of shipping passing up-Channel to the North Sea ports. In the event of an alert, the officers on duty can launch a rescue operation with impressive support from deep-sea tugs and civilian helicopters, as well as the naval rescue force based at Cherbourg. Observant walkers will see plenty of seabirds on the cliffs,

such as gannets or crested cormorants. Nothing manmade seems to bother these birds, not even the barbed wire fences enclosing the rather bleak Beaumont-La Hague nuclear waste reprocessing plant that can be seen at the edge of the deserted heath.

Leaving the shore for a while, you might visit the small community of Jobourg to admire the Roman church, adorned with friezes by Jean-François Millet. Born of a peasant family from Gruchy, Millet studied with Delaroche and settled in Barbizon, a village in north-central France near the Fontainebleau Forest. Several of his beautiful paintings were inspired by his nostalgia for the landscapes around La Hague.

Cap de la Hague

1. Port-Racine, France's smallest port.
2. Cap de la Hague seen from the east, with Saint-Martin and Port-Racine in the foreground.
3. The church and cemetery at Saint-Germain-des-Vaux.
4. Cap de la Hague lighthouse.
5. The village of Les Roches.
6. The coastal path.
7. The semaphore station at Cap de la Hague.
8. Nez de Jobourg and Nez de Voidries.
9. Les Roches village with the tiny port of Goury in the distance.

1	2	3	4
		5	6
7	8	9	

Drystone walls offer some protection from the prevailing winds for crops growing in the fields on Cap de la Hague.

In contrast with the Jobourg cliffs, the long sweeping beach of Vauville Bay is fringed with miles of sand dunes extending almost as far down as Cap Flamanville. The scenery is strikingly dramatic against the restless sea, and because of its rich fauna and flora, the beach, dunes and coastal plain are now a conservation area.

Leaving Beaumont on the road to Vauville, a coastal path on the right leads to the site of Les Pierres Pouquelées, the remains of a megalithic grave gallery. At Vauville you can visit a priory and 16th century castle built in a charming location. Continuing south you pass the commune of Biville and then cross a military firing range to arrive, in due course, at the small port of Diélette.

Once a drying harbour used by fishing boats, Diélette is now a snug marina for up to 400 yachts. On its south side, the harbour is overlooked by traditional stone cottages in true Normandy style, and in summer, ferries take tourists out to the Channel Islands. Until quite recently, an underwater iron mine was worked here, but now a nuclear power plant occupies the site, supplying electricity to the Caen region and part of Brittany. This complex dominates the coast just west of Flamanville village, but somehow doesn't detract from the peace of the area. South of the power station, from high on the dramatic cliffs, you have panoramic views north over the long Vauville beaches, south towards Carteret and seawards to the mysterious profile of Sark. In clear weather you can see all the Channel Islands from this amazing vantage.

The long-distance path, GR223, winds around the headland towards another historic treasure – Flamanville castle. Built in the 17th century by Hervé Bazan, Marquis of Flamanville, this fine, elegantly proportioned residence makes you forget the austere granite rocks surrounding it. The château is set in nearly 20 hectares of parkland, luxuriously planted with palm trees and water features – an exotic, scented haven in the heart of Normandy.

1. Vauville.
2. The dunes and coastal plains of Vauville Bay.
3. Siouville lies at the point where the long beach gives way to the Flamanville cliffs.
4. Cap de Flamanville, with the nuclear power station in the distance.
5. The delightful castle and gardens at Flamanville.
6. Diélette harbour and marina are protected by sturdy breakwaters.
7. Cap du Rozel and Pointe l'Épaule form a rocky promontory jutting out from the straight coast.

1	3
2	
4	5 6
	7

Carteret

Cap de Carteret

Barneville-Plage

Carteret and Portbail

16

1. The beach and dunes north of Carteret.
2 and 3. Carteret is a popular seaside resort from where ferries run to the Channel Islands.
4. Cap de Carteret.
5. The drying harbour at Portbail.
6. Carteret's outer harbour.
7. The inner drying harbour at Carteret

and the marina above the sill.
8. Portbail's fortified church.
9. Cap de Carteret,

the harbour and marina.
10. The tortuous entrance to Portbail.

1	2	3	4	5	8
	6	7	
9	10

South of Flamanville, between Anse de Sciotot and Granville, you can see one of the special geological features of the Cotentin peninsula. The local currents along this long straight coast have created a fantastic stretch of sand dunes, which separate the restless sea and its beaches from the low, marshy areas inland, known locally as *Les Mielles*.

The minor rivers that flow into the sea have a constant battle to prevent their escape routes from becoming choked with sand. The

tidal inlets at Portbail, Saint-Germain-sur-Ay and Regnéville are all partly enclosed by a jutting sand spit, and at low tide each of these wide shallow estuaries becomes a desert of sand threaded with narrow winding channels. Despite their difficult access, the risk of grounding and the physical problems of loading and unloading, coastal schooners plied these tricky natural havens in the days of sail, supporting the economic life of the region. In the past, local peasants came here to collect *tangue*, a mixture of algae and alluvia that was used on the land as a fertilizer.

The stretch of sea separating the west coast of the Cotentin peninsula and the Channel Islands is a notorious passage, swept by strong currents and cluttered with

numerous reefs. Seven miles offshore is the archipelago of Les Écrehou, five square miles of intricate drying reefs and islets. It's perhaps not surprising that seamen through the centuries have given evocative names to dangerous rocks and shoals in this complex sea area. *Banc Fêlés* are the shoals that can quickly break up a hull. *Les Dirouilles* translates as 'the seething reefs' in local patois.

Sheltered by its pronounced headland, Carteret was home to small but tough sailing coasters that traded with the Channel Islands. Even before Carteret had a proper harbour, these boats would dry out on the sands where horse-drawn carts came out to unload them. As it looks today, with its line of quays and port facilities, Carteret dates

Carteret

La Plage

Le Havre   Portbail

from the second half of the 19th century. Over on the south side of the river, Barneville-Plage developed during the Belle Époque when seaside resorts and tourism became popular. Today Carteret and Barneville are part of the same town. Before leaving Carteret, don't miss a stroll along the promenade towards the headland, following the old *Sentier des Douaniers* (Customs Officers' trail) that meanders out around the lighthouse and back past the ruins of a fine old church at Saint-Germain. Recent excavations here have uncovered some ancient graves in a Merovingian place of worship.

'To my right, hills and heath stretched as far as the eye could see. To my left on a rise that dropped quickly to the sea, the crenellated

bell tower of Portbail faded into a grey haze . . .'

Perhaps you will be favoured with better weather than Victor Hugo when he discovered Portbail. You'll probably first notice the charming church of Notre-Dame reflected in the waters of the harbour. Historians have dated the church as 12th century, but it is flanked by a 15th century crenellated tower with a mock defensive parapet. The dual purpose of the tower – religious and military – can be explained by the strategic position of the harbour in the Middle Ages. During the Hundred Years War, a network of towers and fortified belfries (at Barneville, Saint-Georges-de-la-Rivière, Portbail, Saint-Nicolas de Pierrepont) was built to defend this coast against invaders

and provide commanding lookout places.

Excavations in and around Portbail have brought up numerous Gallo-Roman finds – sarcophagi, marble slabs, aqueducts and coins – and in 1956 the foundations of a baptistry were discovered. Its octagonal shape, with a central pool paved with schist, seems oriental, and this has intrigued historians studying the origins of Christianity on the Cotentin peninsula. Portbail's cultural heritage hints at a prestigious past, in contrast to the rather insignificant port we know today.

South of Portbail is a much smaller inlet at Surville. A rocky ledge bars the entrance here, so Surville has never developed as a port. The GR223 path follows the north bank and has views of this

particularly wild place. The coastal belt of dunes and wetlands is a rich wildlife habitat. As well as seabirds and countless tiny avocets, there are plenty of yellowhammers and common linnet around the marshy heath.

The *Conservatoire du littoral et des rivages lacustres* (Coastal Protection Agency) owns fragile areas such as the Lindberg dunes on the south edge of the Portbail estuary, the Hatainville dunes north of Cap Carteret and the land on each bank of the Surville estuary. The agency's compulsory purchase powers help to protect this unique coastline, which is often threatened by proposals for property developments.

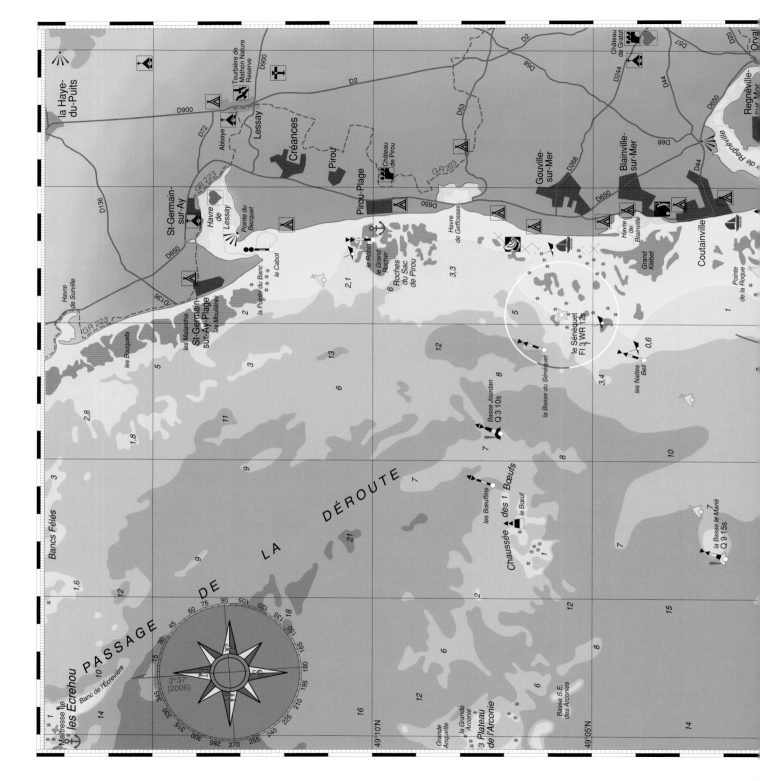

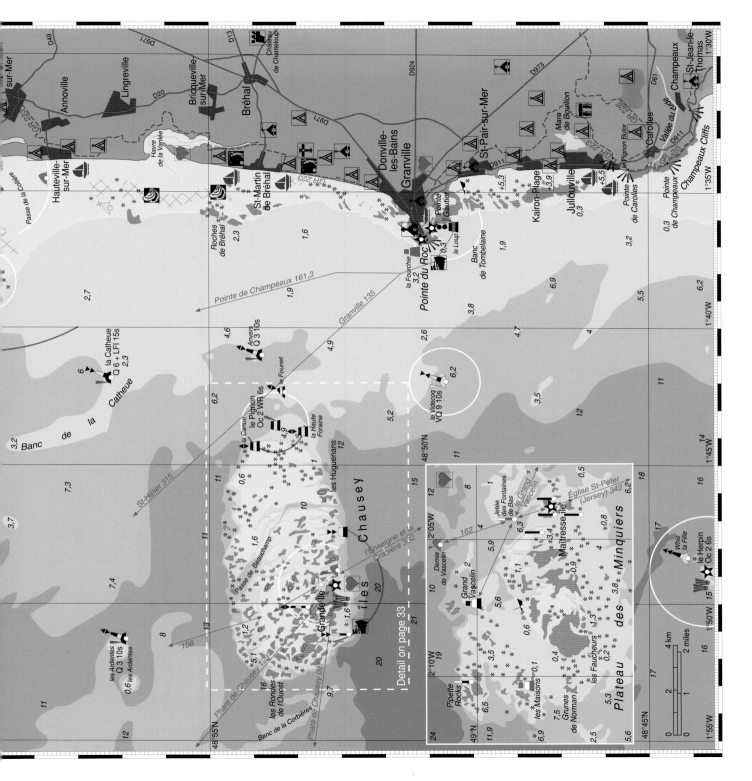

The village of Saint-Germain-sur-Ay is on the north shore of the estuary, which appears to be a sea of mud at low water.

Saint-Germain-sur-Ay-Plage

La pointe du Banc

Pointe du Becquet

Saint-Germain-sur-Ay

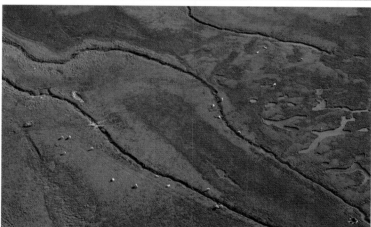

Lessay and Saint-Germain-sur-Ay

The estuaries at Saint-Germain-sur-Ay and Regnéville are the most extensive sandy inlets on the west coast of the Cotentin peninsula. The sinuous River Ay winds past Lessay, then ripples across acres of sands and round Pointe du Becquet before spilling into the sea. Because few boats venture into Saint-Germain-sur-Ay, this vast tidal expanse has remained gloriously wild. The coast path from the north offers a delightful stroll in lovely scenery reminiscent of the wide spaces of the bay of Mont St Michel. The currents are not as strong here and the tide doesn't rise as fast, but the difference in outlook at high and low water is just as striking.

Lessay is probably best known for its historic fair which started in the 12th century and takes place in early September, but the village deserves a visit at any time of year. The Benedictine abbey, built in the 11th and 12th centuries, has seen many conflicts and changes of fortune through the ages, most recently during the Liberation of 1944.

South of Lessay, patchily wooded moorland stretches all the way to Granville. These exposed open plains have always been so infertile that, whenever a piece of land was purchased, a generous tract of the heath was included free of charge. These moors have a haunting beauty as well as being of real ecological importance. The road from Lessay to Coutances crosses the moors from north to south, and footpaths provide an opportunity to explore further.

1. The inlet of Saint-Germain-sur-Ay at low water.
2. Sheep graze the salt marshes at the head of Havre de Saint-Germain.
3. Vauban's hut was built in 1669 as a lookout post, surveying the river entrance near Saint-Germain.
4. The château at Pirou is surrounded by a moat.
5. Pirou-Plage is a fashionable seaside resort.

Continuing south, the soft maritime climate has nurtured an important market gardening industry around Créances. The sandy soils are ideal for vegetable growing, particularly for carrots, leeks, onions, cabbage, parsley, turnips and salsify. There are 2,000 hectares in cultivation here, making Créances the market garden capital of the Cotentin.

The medieval castle at Pirou, two kilometres inland on the D94, is one of the last surviving 12th century fortresses along the English

1		
2	3	4
		5

The haven of Regnéville

The fishermen of Granville, Cancale and the Channel Islands were the first to discover the banks of wild oysters, called les pieds-de-cheval (horse's feet), along the west coast of the Cotentin peninsula. Despite the tradition of solidarity amongst fishermen, there were several disputes over fishing rights. These were eventually resolved by a convention of 1839 regulating the oyster catch.

Channel coast. Its colourful history is as lively as the combative relations between Normandy and old Albion. The castle appears to occupy the site of an ancient Viking entrenchment. Two guard towers and three of the original five defensive gates still exist today, but the drawbridge has been replaced with a stone bridge. There was originally a lake consisting of two wide ponds, but now only the Broc pond remains south of Créances. In a new building on the south side of the castle, the Hauteville Tapestry is on display. Inspired by the Bayeux tapestry, this modern work depicts the exploits of Tancrède de Hauteville in Sicily during the 11th century.

After skirting the small inlet at Blainville, the D651 passes through Coutainville, one of the three largest seaside resorts on this coast. Here, at low tide, the sea uncovers three kilometres of sand, a favourite area for shrimping. Along the foreshore are some unusual stone structures like large Vs on the beach, pointing towards the open sea. These are ancient fish traps, similar to those you can find around the islands off the Charente coast. The Coutainville traps date from the Middle Ages and are still in use today. Shoals of fish swim inshore on the rising tide in search of food, and having satisfied themselves in the shallows, they become trapped in the low stone walls as the tide ebbs. The owners of these fish traps, often local farmers, place

nets across the trap gates before opening them. The fish are washed out by the current, landing in the nets just as if they had been trawled. The catches vary, but some have been so large that one low tide was not enough time to collect all the fish. You can see these strange structures all the way from Granville, past the bay of Mont St Michel to Vivier-sur-Mer. Some are built of stones bound together by wild oysters; others are long fences made of stakes driven into the soil and interwoven with branches.

Built on the dunes, Coutainville has always been vulnerable to very high tides and was flooded several times before sea defences were built at the head of the beach. So far, these walls have been effective. Pointe d'Agon gives a superb

panorama of the open sea into the estuary of the River Sienne, which flows past Regnéville. West of the point as far as Ronquet turret, a vast expanse of mussel beds stretches the entire width of the beach, one of five major shell-fisheries in the Département of Manche. During the Middle Ages, Regnéville was one of the most important ports on the Cotentin peninsula, but commercial activity had declined by the beginning of the 20th century because the entrance and harbour were silting up. The 12th century castle was destroyed by order of Cardinal Richelieu in the early 1600s and today only the four vaulted floors of the square keep remain.

At the head of the estuary, the D20 crosses the River Sienne at Pont-de-la-Roque. Here a few pillars and arches of an ancient bridge survive, once used by local farmers when loading their handcarts with *tangue* and kelp to fertilize the fields. Until the middle of the 19th century, 2,000 handcarts a day arrived from the Cotentin interior to collect the famous 'fertilizer of the sea'.

The Regnéville region is also known for its lime kilns. Limestone was quarried at Montmartin-sur-Mer to make fertilizer or building material. The Coast and Limestone Museum (*Musée du Littoral et de la Chaux*) demonstrates this old industry using models and original tools. You can also visit the lime kilns at Rey, on the road between Regnéville and Montmartin, which are part of the museum.

Before leaving the Regnéville

The haven of Regnéville

1. Pointe d'Agon lighthouse.
2. Meadows near Regnéville.
3. Low-water work on the mussel beds is carried out with tractors.
4. Regnéville-sur-Mer and the estuary.
5. The boatyard near Regnéville-sur-Mer.
6. The wild estuary at Blainville.
7. The lighthouse and Pointe d'Agon at low water.
8. Harvesting the catch from a Cotentin fish trap.

region you should visit Coutances, whose old town centre, well-preserved buildings and ancient courtyards bear witness to its history, despite the damage suffered in several wars. This small town played a pivotal role in the numerous conflicts between Brittany and Normandy. The crowning glory of Coutances is its magnificent Gothic cathedral, one of Normandy's architectural jewels. The cathedral has an octagonal tower whose windows illuminate the transept crossing.

1	2	4		5
3				
6		7		8

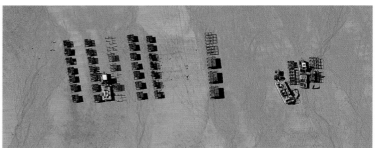

The haven of Vanlée

1. The haven of Vanlée, from the south. Bottom right is the hamlet of Salines, reached by a few intrepid boats up its winding channel.
2. The vast expanse of mussel beds off Vanlée. Work starts even before low water is reached.
3. Towards the top of the beach are the cages in which the young mussels are reared.
4. At Donville-les-Bains, just north of Granville, you can see the V-shaped fish traps through the crystal-clear water.

Travelling south from Regnéville past Hauteville-sur-Mer, you skirt the inlet of Vanlée before reaching Bréhal. Vanlée is the last tidal estuary on this part of the coast and probably the wildest of them all. As such it is now a protected site. The sandbanks are startlingly white and the dunes protecting the haven are bare of any habitation; only the tiny hamlet of Salines borders the east bank. Across the middle of the inlet, a tidal causeway links Bréhal to Saint-Martin-de-Bréhal.

Before reaching Granville, visit the moated castle at Chanteloup about two kilometres east of Bréhal. The fine long beaches of the west coast of the Cotentin come to an abrupt end at Granville, where the rocky headland of Pointe du Roc gives a hint of what to expect along the Brittany coast.

Granville marks the southern boundary of what geologists call *La Côte des Havres*. Here, the long procession of dunes and marshes bisected by small estuaries is broken by the rocky headlands of Granville and Carolles. This sudden appearance of granite and schist heralds the proximity of Brittany and extends towards the open sea and the Chausey Islands. For walkers as well as for navigators, these scattered rocks and steep cliffs provide a change of scene from the sandy marches of west Cotentin.

Granville is the main port on this coast, its interests entirely orientated towards the sea. Here is a large sheltered yacht marina, a busy fishing harbour and a well-known spa. Granville's reputation as a sailing centre and the riches of its maritime history are brought together by a project to rebuild the traditional lugger *La Granvillaise*. Perched on the headland of Pointe du Roc, the old quarter of Granville overlooks the harbour and the sea. This part of town is fascinating to explore, with its narrow streets and alleys lined with 16th and 17th century houses. These fine buildings, the commanding ramparts and the great gateways into the old town have assured Granville a place on the list of protected heritage sites.

Within the ramparts of the upper town, you can trace more then five centuries of history. It was the English who first fortified the Pointe du Roc in the 15th century. Strategically this headland was an ideal base for an assault on the coveted Mont St Michel. English troops actually dug a deep trench which could be flooded by the sea to transform the camp on Pointe du Roc into an island. Despite this, they were defeated by the defenders of the Mont St Michel in 1442.

Granville really started to flourish after being granted a coat of arms by the charter of Charles VII, which also gave Norman settlers in Granville exemption from taxes. The upper city developed along two main streets and around the church of Notre-Dame. From the south rampart, on Boulevard des Terre-Neuviers and in

1. The prominent headland of Pointe du Roc, with Granville harbour and marina on its south side.
2. Granville's Grande-Porte, the main entrance into the walled town, was built in 1630.
3. The traditional lugger *La Granvillaise*, under spectacular full sail.
4. Gathering whelks on the rocky shore near low water.
5. The houses of the upper town are built right up to the north ramparts on Pointe du Roc.
6. Some of the bold and flamboyant villas of the upper town overlook the port.

Granville

	1	
2	3	

1. Looking north over the old town with the church of Notre-Dame, built in granite from Chausey, on the left.
2. At the foot of Pointe du Roc are the sea-water spa, in the old Normandy Hotel, and the Granville casino. The buildings were designed by the Parisian architect Auguste Bluysen and built in 1911.
3. The sea breaks over the Normandy Hotel in strong north-westerly weather.

particular Place de l'Œuvre, you have an incredible view over the port and town. In this historic quarter there are several small parks and gardens and also the museums of Vieux Granville and Richard-Anacréon.

From the old barracks, now a car park, you can walk around Pointe du Roc. After following a low wall, take the old lookouts route towards the lighthouse, which was built in 1827. The white light flashes three times every 15 seconds with a range of 22 miles. The panoramic view takes in the Cotentin coast and the Chausey Islands eight miles offshore, but Mont St Michel is hidden by the Carolles cliffs. Steps lead down from the lighthouse to the shore, passing round Cap Lihou. The sea breaks around the rocky base of the lighthouse and you can still see the

walls of ancient fish traps and rows of oyster beds. During the summer at low tide, locals and visitors come to gather whelks and other shellfish along the rocky foreshore.

Partly sheltered from the prevailing winds by Pointe du Roc, Granville was one of the great cod ports of the French Channel coast, along with Fécamp, St Malo and Paimpol, whose fishermen sailed away for months to the fishing grounds of Iceland and Newfoundland. Granville's fleet of about 100 deep-sea fishing boats, with over 2,500 crew, was financed to a great extent by Jewish jewellers and bankers who settled in the town after leaving Spain at the end of the 15th century. This fishing declined in the early 1900s and had virtually ceased by the Second World War.

Before the fleet set off to the North Atlantic, Granville always held a three-day carnival. The boats were decked out with flags and the crews and their families wore masks and costumes, before the long months of separation. Every February, Granville still celebrates with a carnival, the only reminder of this period in the town's history.

Granville has three port basins. The outer drying harbour is protected by the breakwater built in 1778, and here the boats sink gently into soft mud on each low tide. There is a locked basin for small cargo vessels, and for the trawlers which unload their catches alongside the fish market. In 1978 a large marina for about 1,000 boats was built in the Hérel basin, accessible above half tide through a sill gate.

	1	
4	5	6
	2	3

HALLE A MAREE

1. Sheltered by the cliffs of Pointe du Roc is the harbour at Granville, with Port Hérel marina in the foreground.

2. The futuristic fish market on the inner-harbour quay.

3. Fishing boats dried out by the west breakwater for scrubbing.

4. A trawler alongside the quay.

5. The entrance to the marina at low water showing the retaining sill.

6. The lock between the commercial inner harbour and the outer drying harbour.

Granville to Pointe de Carolles

1. The beach and resort of Saint-Pair-sur-Mer.
2. The beach at Jullouville, with Bouillon lake in the distance.
3. Traditional beach huts at Carolles.
4. At Pointe de Carolles, the Pignon Butor rock marks the opening of the beautiful Valley of the Painters.
5. The beach at Carolles has a lifeguard tower.
6. The orientation table on Pointe de Carolles. The panorama stretches from Granville to Pointe du Grouin and in clear weather you can see Îles Chausey.

For a few kilometres south of Granville, the landscape reverts from rock to sandy beaches and dunes. The charming resorts of Saint-Pair, Édenville, Kairon, Jullouville and Carolles are favourite French holiday destinations, and Granville itself was one of the first tourist resorts in France.

In the early 1800s, most visitors to the seaside were seeking some kind of cure, having heard of the restorative effects of fresh air and sea bathing. Adverts of the period made extravagant claims about the benefits to weak constitutions of breathing air rich in iodine from the kelp and lichen on the rocky shoreline. The first bathing huts were built at Granville in 1828, well before those at Deauville or Biarritz.

With the opening of Granville casino in 1858, the resorts of Plat Gousset, Saint-Pair and Carolles became very prosperous. This was helped in no small measure by visits from celebrities of the day such as Michelet, Stendhal and Victor Hugo. The success of these resorts spawned the idea of excursions by train from Paris to Granville, and as soon as the good weather arrived each season, these popular trips would start.

Today you can still find these now highly desirable 'retro' bathing huts in a line along the beach at Carolles. Contemporary tourists want smart hotels with fitness suites, tennis courts, golf courses and equestrian centres, so facilities have changed since the early days. Beaches now have lifeguard stations, launching slips for boats and surfboards, and supervised activities for youngsters.

The beaches in this area shelve very gradually, and at low spring tides the sea might be a kilometre and a half away, leaving great expanses of sand and rocky plateaux which shellfish gatherers enjoy. You can find several old stone fish traps and here, close to the bay of Mont St Michel, flounder are particularly abundant. Along this stretch of coast dredging for oysters is a traditional seasonal activity, particularly the

famous flat oysters, *pieds-de-cheval*, found near Pointe du Roc. Apart from the coastline itself, which is most attractive, the towns of Saint-Pair, Jullouville and Carolles have little of architectural note. One exception is the parish church at Saint-Pair, which has an elegant Romanesque stone spire.

South of the resort of Carolles-Plage, just where the beautiful Champeaux cliffs begin, two small valleys meet the sea. The 'Valley of the Painters' is carved out by a winding stream known as Le Crapeu, a peaceful and picturesque place still popular with artists. The wild Lude Valley with its steep cliffs either side, emerges at the foot of Sard Rock. This stream rises just a few kilometres from the coast, north of Champeaux village, and its pleasant

valley has preserved its rich natural habitat. Legend has it that Satan had taken refuge on Sard Rock, also called the Devil's Chair, when a stroke of Saint Michael's sword opened up the valley. You can explore this area from the car park at Pignon Butor by following the coastal path, part of the GR223, either north towards the beach of St Michel or south to Saint-Jean-le-Thomas.

Walking along the cliff path opens up magnificent vistas across the bay of Mont St Michel. The path passes through a rich mixture of ferns, alders and iris, and you might surprise small mammals near their burrows. The Lude tumbles over a mass of rocks and boulders to reach the sea. Known as the Lude Gateway, this wild-looking

The Champeaux Cliffs and the Lude Valley

1. The wooded cliffs of Champeaux. The coastal footpath follows the old excise men's trail 60m above the sea, offering spectacular views. This area is known locally as 'the most beautiful kilometre of France'.
2 and 3. Signs for the footpath and the bird reserve.
4. Built in the 17th century, Vauban's cabin was used as an early-warning lookout for enemy ships approaching the bay.
5. A landing slip at the bottom of the cliffs near Saint-Jean-le-Thomas.

landscape was used as a hideout during the Chouan revolt, a pro-royalist uprising in the 1790s. Most of the Chouan army were young men from the country north of the Loire. Today the Lude Valley is part of Carolles' historic heritage and the stream is maintained by a local preservation society and a bird-watching group.

29

The Plateau des Minquiers

1. At low water, acres of rippling sandbanks are exposed.
2 and 3. On Maîtresse Île, the only island with any vegetation, are half a dozen cottages, mostly belonging to Jersey islanders who live in them in the summer.
4. The famous Minquiers toilet, the most southerly convenience in the British Isles.
5. The stone plaque claiming the islands as part of the States of Jersey. Erected in the 1930s, it was the focus of the long-running dispute over sovereignty between France and Britain.

'Les Minquiers – a chilling black hole on the chart!' is how the French hydrographic engineer Charles Rollet described this notorious expanse of reefs, and he knew what he was talking about. In 1888, Rollet was given the task of surveying the most hostile rocky plateau in the English Channel. 'A lonely wilderness' proclaims Victor Hugo in *Toilers of the Sea*, written during his years of exile in Guernsey.

Today, fishermen from St Malo or Granville more prosaically assert that the best way to cross Les Minquiers is first to drink a bottle of rum, then close your eyes. Yet despite these introductions, there's something compelling about this spooky archipelago that can draw mariners in close just to have a look.

Lying six nautical miles north-west of Chausey, 15 miles north of St Malo and nine miles south of Jersey, the Plateau des Minquiers is a vast maze of drying reefs, rocky heads and gravel banks almost the size of Jersey itself. The area enclosed by its six cardinal buoys exceeds 100 square miles and a cruise around the buoyed perimeter would cover 43 miles. To cap it all, this fantastic tangle of dangers is scoured by the most extravagant tides in Europe. The spring range here can reach 11 metres and streams may touch six knots locally.

In contrast to Chausey, Les Minquiers has only one 'green' island – Maîtresse Île – sheltered from the highest tides. The other islets of any size, such as Les Maisons or Les Faucheurs, are exposed to the worst of the elements. Even so, at high water Maîtresse Île is barely 200 metres long by 40 metres wide! This didn't stop half a dozen small cottages of modest comfort being built here at the end of the 19th century. Most belong to Jersey islanders, who use them in the summer. Maîtresse Île has no facilities, nothing to visit and nowhere to walk. But yachtsmen who dare penetrate its cordon of reefs never forget the peace of this lonely island, where hundreds of sea-birds take refuge.

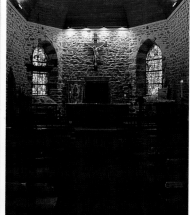

The islands and reefs of the Chausey archipelago are more compact than the scattered rocky chaos of Les Minquiers. On a chart, Chausey plateau is almost a perfect oval, extending six miles from east to west and just over two miles north to south. Washed by the greatest tides in Europe, Îles Chausey are the jewels of the Bay of St Malo. Several navigable channels wind through the archipelago, used by yachts and fishing boats in quiet weather.

In summer, tourist boats regularly come out to Grande Île from Granville. Spring tides are the most dramatic time to visit. Then, at low water, much of the plateau dries out to a maze of rocks, sand pools and winding channels. Apart from its narrow entrance from the south,

the natural harbour in Chausey Sound is practically landlocked for several hours until the flood returns.

Grande Île has a hotel-restaurant, a small general store and bar, and a few holiday cottages. From just above the landing place, a sandy track leads out to the lighthouse where, on a clear day, you can see the cliffs east of St Malo between Pointe du Meinga and Pointe du Grouin before the land drops away towards Mont St Michel.

Chausey has a calm atmosphere of peaceful independence, cocooned from the outside world by its natural barrier of rock and sand. Entering the archipelago is like crossing a frontier into a magical private domain. The climate is soft down here in the Bay of St Malo, and most depressions from the Atlantic

pass further north through the English Channel. Chausey is also well protected from heavy seas, by the French mainland to the east and south, and by Jersey and Les Minquiers to the north and west.

The archipelago is also a paradise of safe habitats for shellfish, seabirds, puffins and sometimes seals. Much of Grand Île is privately owned, except for a small public section at the south of the island around Pointe de la Tour, which has been part of the commune of Granville since 1802. *La Société*

The Chausey Archipelago

1. Grande Île and the northern Chausey archipelago at high water, most of the rocky shoals and sandbanks are submerged.
2. Looking north-west along the east coast of Grande Île, with the drying anchorage at Blainvillais.
3. Inside the chapel on Grande Île.
4. The chapel on Chausey was built in the 1850s on a small hill above Anse des Blainvillais.
5. Chausey's lighthouse, at the east end of Grande Île, has a range of 23 nautical miles.

1		
2	3	4
		5

The Chausey Archipelago

1. L'Anse du Pont and Gros Mont harbour, at the north end of the island where the islanders over-winter their boats.
2 The mirror images of the beaches of Grande-Grève and Port-Homard either side of the south-east point of Grande Île.

3. Boats and dories in Anse du Pont at high water.
4. Traditional cottages overlooking Blainvillais beach.

5. *La Cancalaise* sailing up the Sound.
6. The cove at the foot of Marin-Marie's house.

7. The muddy foreshore of the Sound near low water.
8. Dory racing off Chausey.

Civile Immobilière (SCI) was founded in 1919 by four local families, to trace the freeholds and history of property ownership in Chausey.

As with all the islands in the Bay of St Malo, Chausey has had a chequered and colourful history as England, France and the old Duchy of Normandy have claimed possession at some time or other. In 1763, the Treaty of Paris ceded to Britain control over what we now call the Channel Islands, plus the Plateau des Minquiers. France retained Îles Chausey, which are sometimes known as the French Channel Islands. Down through the centuries, Saxon pirates, smugglers, utopian farmers, crooked innkeepers, monks, mad scientists and frayed industrialists have escaped to the archipelago, drawn by its isolation for their very different reasons.

The story of Grande Île's old castle – Château de Matignon – is part of this history. Built in 1559, it was destroyed several times by English invaders. Abandoned for almost 200 years, the castle was finally restored between 1922 and 1924 by the French motor car magnate Louis Renault, who loved to escape to Chausey from the hectic world of manufacturing.

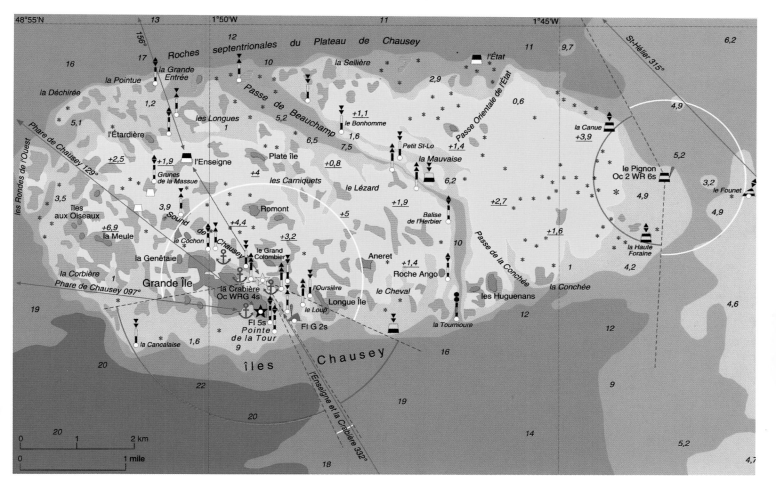

As the chart shows, most of the plateau is exposed at low spring tides, when several square miles of seabed can be explored on foot! The central part is a spectacular mosaic of golden sand, soft mud and heaped banks of shingle and crushed shells, all strewn with jagged granite, carpets of kelp and tiny green islands. French visitors often range across this enticing expanse, looking for clams in the sand, mussels on the rocks, and crabs or lobsters in hidden pools.

Chausey has more real 'islands' than Les Minquiers, and at dead low water when the streams are slack you can get to many of them either in a dinghy or simply by walking across from Grande Île. Île Longue is on the south edge of the plateau, half a mile east of Pointe de la Tour and an easy landing in calm conditions. Aneret is a good mile east of Grande Île and only visited by locals who know their way.

L'Enseigne is familiar to mariners because of its black-and-white beacon which, lined up with the top of La Tour lighthouse, leads safely into the archipelago from the north-north-west. At low-water springs, L'Enseigne is surrounded by firm sand and, except during the bird-breeding season, when landing on the small islands is prohibited, you can stroll out here from the north end of Grande Île.

In the old days, quarrymen and seaweed gatherers used these islets and you can still see the ruins of small cottages beneath the vegetation, particularly on Île Longue. On a really low tide, observant explorers can gaze upon a strange pattern of granite blocks, a kind of submarine stone circle 12 metres in diameter. This eerie megalith is said to be the foundation of an ancient tomb, some 7,000 years old.

The west side of the plateau is the wildest and most exposed to storms, with only a few islets that are always above water – Le Chapeau, La Massue, La Meule and Îles aux Oiseaux. It's best to explore this area by dinghy on a warm still day, when you can look down into the clear channels and watch small fish darting about.

Chausey, Grande Île

Marin-Marie, painter, writer and yachtsman, spent much of his time at his home on Grande Île, Chausey, close to the island's chapel, where he had a magnificent studio facing the Sound. His deep love of the islands and his understanding of the sea produced numerous masterpieces. In the 1930s he twice crossed the Atlantic single-handed.

1. The massive tidal range and the vast sandbanks are ideal for oyster cultivation. Close to the largest of the Huguenans islands, you can see rows of stakes on which young oysters are reared.

2. Grande Île's old castle – Château de Matignon – is now known as Château Renault. After nearly 200 years' neglect it was finally restored in the 1920s by the French motor car magnate Louis Renault, who loved to escape to Chausey.

3. A maze of islets, rocks, channels and sand banks. The Huguenans islands and La Conchée islet are in the foreground.

4. The sandbanks and rock pools around the Chausey islands are a paradise for cockling and winkling.

5. Aneret Island, to the east of Grande Île, has a small cottage.

1	3
	4
2	5

Chausey Archipelago

1. The southern part of Grande Île and the Sound. It is barely half-tide and already most of the rocks and islands are connected by sand-banks.
2 to 5. The gradually changing seascape of the Sound, as a big spring tide ebbs away.

As the tide falls, sandbanks provide sheltered anchorages, as you can see here in amongst Les Trois Îles.

THE VERSATILE DORIES

The highly practical dories of Chausey are descended from the famous boats used by Granville cod fishermen off Newfoundland. These flat-bottomed boats were stacked on the decks of the schooners as they set off for the North Atlantic. Six or seven metres long with a shallow draught and pretty sheer, dories are ideally suited to conditions around Chausey.

Islanders use these versatile little boats for laying their crab pots, for line or net fishing, for a beach trip with the family or for collecting parcels or supplies at the quay. Until recently, you would see dories everywhere around the islands, but now the best opportunity is at the local regatta on 15th August each year.

Although, to some visitors, Chausey can feel exposed to the elements, it's amazing how much natural shelter is provided by this complex tangle of rock, sand and shingle. In this respect Grande Île seems perfectly placed on the south side of the plateau. In south-westerly gales there is no great fetch of sea, with the Brittany mainland only about 15 miles upwind. In strong westerlies Grande Île itself protects Chausey Sound, which is completely snug until the wind veers round to the north-west and worries the harbour side of the island. But even in hard north-westerlies, two miles of natural rock and sand protect the Sound, taking the weight of any seas that build up in the short distance between Chausey and Les Minquiers.

The most spectacular form of shelter comes from the ebbing tide, when acres of rock and sand are gradually exposed to shut out the restless sea and leave the residual channels as peaceful as a man-made harbour enclosed by piers. The rise and fall of tide can be 12 metres at the top of springs, a fantastic difference in sea level equivalent to the combined height of three double-decker buses!

On a low spring tide in Chausey, the rocks along the east edge of the Sound loom high above the anchorage like fortress walls and your boat lies perfectly sheltered in an almost landlocked lagoon. Then you can take the dinghy ashore and wander among fascinating reefs, untouched stretches of sand, limpid rock pools and winding channels which, only a few hours before, were submerged under megatons of fast-moving water.

The tranquillity of this exposed wilderness place is truly restful and you can reckon on maybe three hours of complete peace – an hour and a half each side of low tide – before fingers of tide start creeping back among the reefs. Then the channels steadily widen and spill over to join small pools into larger pools, and large pools into gleaming expanses that meet behind islands and steadily shrink the warm tracts of sand until, without you really noticing, the seabed has disappeared again beneath the brimming flood.

The Bay of Mont St Michel

On the cusp between Brittany and Normandy, the Bay of Mont St Michel is a unique, dramatic seascape. Sheer cliffs at each end embrace vast acres of sand and mud which cover and uncover hypnotically with each tide. The geometric patterns of oyster beds on the sands give way to mudflats with abundant wildlife, then salt marshes, and finally lush meadows where sheep graze. Beyond the fertile coastal fringe, small shady valleys meander inland. The famous landmark of Mont St Michel rises majestically from the edge of the sands, lapped by the sea at high tide. Within that great inlet between Pointe du Grouin and the Champeaux cliffs, the flat sands and marshes of the Bay of Mont St Michel stretch as far as the eye can see. The muted colours of the sea, the muddy sand and the lonely marshes often merge in haze to create a strangely mystical landscape. Over the centuries, man and nature have achieved a striking equilibrium on this special part of the coast. The rhythm of tides and seasons ensures a rich variety of wildlife, while in this apparently fragile environment, one of the architectural jewels of history has been built – the haunting silhouette of Mont St Michel.

1. Mont St Michel and Tombelaine Rock look like two ships dried out on the sands, waiting for the tide.
2. Saint Michael vanquishing the Devil.

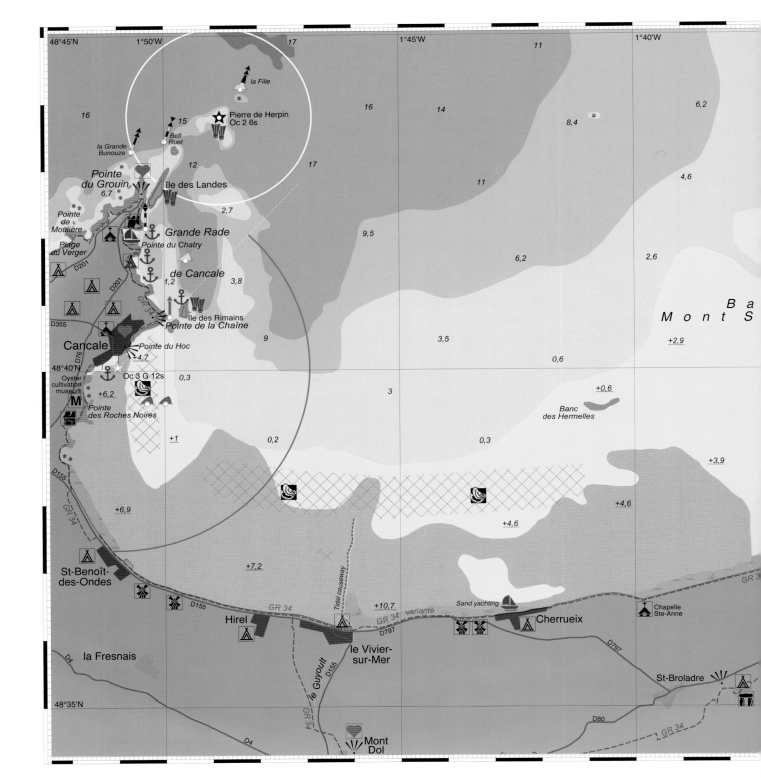

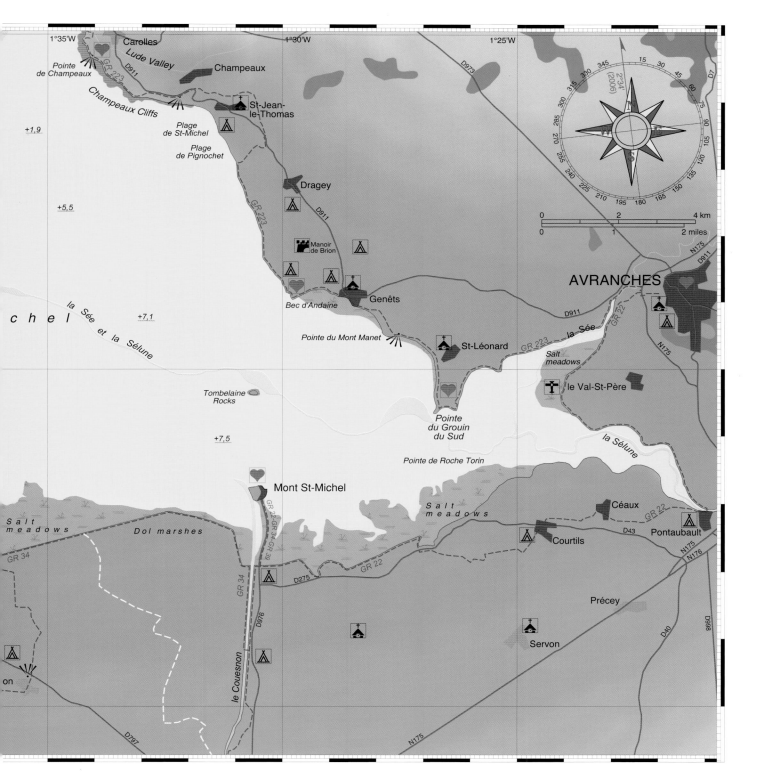

1°35'W   1°30'W   1°25'W

Carolles

Lude Valley

Champeaux

Pointe
de Champeaux

GR 223

D911

Champeaux Cliffs

St-Jean-
le-Thomas

Plage
de St-Michel

+1,9

Plage
de Pignochet

+5,5

Dragey

GR 223

D911

Manoir
de Brion

+7,1

c h e l

la Sée et la Sélune

Bec d'Andaine

Genêts

Pointe du Mont Manet

St-Léonard

GR 223

la Sée

Salt
meadows

GR 22

AVRANCHES

D911

D973

N175

D911

N175

le Val-St-Père

Tombelaine
Rocks

Pointe
du Grouin
du Sud

la Sélune

+7,5

Pointe de Roche Torin

Mont St-Michel

Salt
meadows

Céaux

GR 22

Salt
meadows

Dol marshes

GR 22 GR 34 GR 39

Courtils

D43

Pontaubault

N175

GR 34

D275

GR 22

N176

le Couesnon

GR 34

D976

Précey

N175

D40

D998

on

Servon

D797

N175

2°34'
(2006)

0   2   4 km
0   1   2 miles

D7

Around the Bay of Mont St Michel

1. The village of Saint-Jean-le-Thomas.
2. The long sandy beach of Pignochet, south of Saint-Jean-le-Thomas.
3. The distant outline of Mont St Michel.
4. The church and cemetery of Dragey.
5. Manoir de Brion was built in the 12th century as a Benedictine priory.
6. An old anchor on a gable end in Dragey.

The Bay of Mont St Michel merges softly with the mainland as immense tracts of sand gradually give way to salt marshes. On high spring tides, the sea pours over these coastal fringes, then abandons them again to sheep, barnacle geese and widgeon. The bay itself has a fine sediment rich in calcium carbonate, locally called tangue. Three small rivers – the Sée, Sélune and Couesnon – carve sweeping curves in the sand which are obliterated by the next tide.

The 19th century historian Jules Michelet wrote of this great bay: 'Imagine a great plain of white ash, a dubious kind of sand whose deceptive softness is a dangerous trap.'

The cliffs of Pointe de Champeaux end abruptly at Saint-Jean-le-Thomas where the tiny Mill Brook spills out. This charming village, with its pretty south-facing holiday villas, is well known for its warm microclimate and used to be called the Nice of the English Channel. It is here that the Bay of Mont St Michel really begins. At low tide, the flat coastline reveals wide stretches of sand where a few shellfisheries still work. Lonely dunes fringe the beach all the way to Bec d'Andaine, where the salt meadows begin, locally called *herbus*. The best way to discover this coast is by following the minor road from Saint-Jean-le-Thomas to Genêts, which passes through Obrey and Launay and close to the Manoir de Brion. Running between the D911 and the coast, this route has beauti-

ful views over the marshes and the dunes across the bay. Walkers can continue following the GR223 coastal path, which is well marked.

On the beaches of Saint-Michel and Pignochet, near Saint-Jean-le-Thomas, you might be surprised to see a village of small bungalows. The original structures were built on the dunes by beach fishermen for storing their equipment, but in the early 1900s, as seaside holidays became more popular, these huts were gradually transformed into beach cabins. With the introduction of paid annual holidays in the 1930s, the cabins became genuine holiday bungalows. These little dolls' houses are a quaint local curiosity.

At Vains-Saint-Léonard, not far from Pointe du Grouin du Sud, you can visit the Maison de la Pêche à

Pied (Cockling and Winkling Museum), where an exhibition of paintings, photos, tools and machinery shows the different techniques used in the bay for this type of fishing. A 19th century salt works has been restored to demonstrate another traditional practice.

During the era of religious pilgrimages, this tiny village on the edge of the bay received plenty of visitors. From Bec d'Andaine, the faithful would set off across the sands to reach Mont St Michel. The six-kilometre crossing was often dangerous owing to the speed of the flood tide and the quicksands (known locally as *lises*) which present a very real danger. Quicksand can form when hollows or pools fill with sand suspended in water,

which may happen in corners where a river channel changes course. In the 19th century, 30 or 40 people would get stuck every year. Whilst serious accidents are now rare, there is still a risk today, so you should always take an experienced guide when venturing onto the bay on foot.

Not far east of Bec d'Andaine, Genêts was once a convenient port for shipping supplies across to the Mont St Michel. Granite from the quarries on Chausey would be brought across to the mainland before being taken to the Mont to build the abbey. In the Middle Ages, Genêts was an easily accessible port on the Lerre estuary, but sand gradually encroached, blocking the river. Now the village is cut off from the sea by dunes and salt marshes.

Around the Bay of Mont St Michel

1. Bec d'Andaine and the great expanse of sand that cut off the old port at Genêts.
2. The village of Genêts where many people start their

An interpretation centre at Genêts, La Maison de la Baie, explains the natural history of this amazing inlet and the guided walks across the bay start here.

Between Genêts and Bec d'Andaine, the Manoir de Brion was built as a Benedictine priory attached to Mont St Michel. During the 12th century, many pilgrims, including royalty, stayed here before crossing to the Mont. Visitors can again have this unique experience as the present owners offer *chambre d'hôte* in the old manor house.

crossings to the Mont.
3. Pointe du Grouin du Sud deep in the bay, just on the start of the flood.
4. The church and cemetery at Genêts.
5. The old priory of Saint–Léonard.
6. A horse and cart creating a wake as they cross the bay.
7. Tombelaine Rock is a bird sanctuary.

1	2	
3	4	5
	6	7

Around the Bay of Mont St Michel

1. The ramparts and old quarter of Avranches escaped bombardment during the Liberation.
2. Mont St Michel and the causeway at high tide.
3. Frescoes at the Avranches Botanical Gardens.
4. The old quarter of Avranches.
5. The Botanical Gardens at Avranches shelter many rare plant species.
6. A traditional apple cart, a reminder that

Normandy is cider country.

1	
3 4	2
5 6	

Out in the bay, about halfway between Bec d'Andaine and Mont St Michel, Tombelaine rock is a granite outcrop about 56 metres high. A chapel dedicated to Sainte-Marie-la-Gisante was built on this little islet, but in the 17th century Superintendent Fouquet, who owned Tombelaine at the time, transformed the chapel into a castle. It was later razed to the ground on the orders of Louis XIV and today nothing remains except a few ruins covered by scrub. Tombelaine is now a bird sanctuary for numerous migratory species.

High on a hill on the south bank of the River Sée, Avranches overlooks the bay of Mont St Michel. Parts of the old town were authentically reconstructed after the damage wrought during the Liberation, but most of the town was rebuilt in the post-war style. Avranches is a fascinating town to visit. Don't miss the church of Saint-Gervais, a walk around the Botanical Gardens, or a visit to see the famous manuscripts of Mont St Michel Abbey.

The leafy valley of the Sélune River is rich in flora and fauna. There are hydroelectric barrages at Roche-qui-Boit and Vezins, each with an impressive reservoir behind. The river rises close to Saint-Cyr-du-Bailleul and joins the River Sée south-west of Avranches before flowing into the bay. Passing through the village of Ducey, it flows under a fine 17th century bridge which is illuminated on summer nights.

Legend has it that Saint Aubert, Bishop of Avranches in 709, had three dreams telling him to build a sanctuary on Mont Tombe, a rock in the bay now known as the Bay of Mont St Michel. The sanctuary was dedicated to the archangel Saint Michel and monks went to the island to pray to him. The Mont soon became a place of pilgrimage. In the 10th century the monks of the Mont started to build the abbey on the island and a village grew up on the lower slopes. Throughout the Middle Ages the reputation of the abbey grew, as did the number of pilgrims. By the 16th century the great church at the rock's summit, a cloister and a refectory on the west slope of the island were built.

During the French Revolution, the Benedictine monks were evicted and Mont St Michel was used as a prison, a practice which continued until 1863. The now famous rock was classified as a historic monument in 1874 and major restoration work was undertaken. The Mont has been open to the public since the late 1800s. A new monastic community, followers of Saint Benoît, was re-established on the Mont in 1969 and ten years later this extraordinary place was listed by UNESCO as a World Heritage Site.

Visitors to Mont St Michel enter through three successive gates – Porte de l'Avancée, Porte du Boulevard and Porte du Roi – before coming into La Grande Rue, which is lined with shops just as it was in the Middle Ages. The oldest houses are half-timbered and were built in the 15th and 16th centuries. There are two churches within the abbey but, because of the shape of the rock itself, the architecture and layout of the cloisters and buildings do not conform to the traditional layout of other Benedictine monasteries.

The museums let you discover 1,000 years of complex history, looking at the Mont's architecture, its life as a prison and the notorious dungeons. The Archéoscope gives a religious perspective of the Mont, while the Sea and Ecology Museum explains the working of the tides and the dynamics of the bay's special ecosystem. On summer evenings, a spectacular son et lumière presents an evocative description of the life of Mont St Michel.

Mont St Michel

43

1. Mont St Michel, looking back towards the mainland.
2, 3 and 4. Views from the walls towards the summit of Mont St Michel.
5. A monastic tableau in the cloisters.

1	
2	3	4	5

The Bay of Mont St Michel

1. On the west side of the bay, thousands of oysters are reared.
2. On the southern side of the bay, hundreds of acres of land have been reclaimed from the sea since the mid 19th century.
3. Flocks of sheep graze the salt marshes, producing the delicately flavoured lamb *prés-salés*, an important contributor to the local economy

THE WORLD'S LARGEST TIDES
The west coast of the Cotentin and the Channel Islands experience the biggest tides in Europe. In the Bay of Mont St Michel, the difference between low and high water on a big spring tide can reach 15 metres, more than the height of three double-decker buses. It may be a local cliché to say that the tide comes in at the speed of a galloping horse, but it will certainly outpace even a fast walker across the sands. Watching a spring flood tide from the ramparts of the Mont or out on the Pointe de Grouin du Sud, the speed of the surging bore is mesmerizing.

This spectacular sweeping expanse covers 500 square kilometres. As the tide retreats, it leaves behind an immense area of sand crossed by the winding channels of the Sée, the Sélune and the Couesnon rivers. On its shores is the largest acreage of salt meadows in France, bordered by marshes and land reclaimed from the sea. During the 19th century, Dutch engineers helped create these polders and they were also involved with canalizing the Couesnon River.

The bay is an important habitat for the English Channel and North Sea, because very young flatfish grow here, particularly sole and plaice. It is also a staging post for many species of migratory fish and

an area much appreciated by dolphins. Vast numbers of migrating and indigenous birds are also an essential part of this ecosystem. Economically, the bay claims to have the largest flocks (about 7,000) of salt meadow sheep in France, and it produces up to 10,000 tons of mussels and 3,000 tons of oysters annually. Cuttlefish and shrimps are also gathered here in large quantities. But perhaps the most significant contributors to the local economy are the two million or more tourists who visit the Mont every year.

1	2
	3

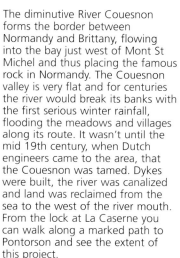
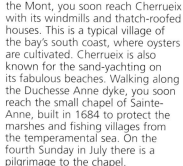

Le Couesnon, Pontorson, Cherrueix

The diminutive River Couesnon forms the border between Normandy and Brittany, flowing into the bay just west of Mont St Michel and thus placing the famous rock in Normandy. The Couesnon valley is very flat and for centuries the river would break its banks with the first serious winter rainfall, flooding the meadows and villages along its route. It wasn't until the mid 19th century, when Dutch engineers came to the area, that the Couesnon was tamed. Dykes were built, the river was canalized and land was reclaimed from the sea to the west of the river mouth. From the lock at La Caserne you can walk along a marked path to Pontorson and see the extent of this project.

Back on the shore to the west of

the Mont, you soon reach Cherrueix with its windmills and thatch-roofed houses. This is a typical village of the bay's south coast, where oysters are cultivated. Cherrueix is also known for the sand-yachting on its fabulous beaches. Walking along the Duchesse Anne dyke, you soon reach the small chapel of Sainte-Anne, built in 1684 to protect the marshes and fishing villages from the temperamental sea. On the fourth Sunday in July there is a pilgrimage to the chapel.

Looking out to sea from here you can identify the Hermelles bank, a surprising natural reef in the sand. This curious feature is formed of tiny calcium tubes secreted by the honeycomb worm, *Sabellaria alveolata*, which shelters and finds food there. Older locals can

remember this bank being over two metres high, but today it barely reaches a metre. The finely balanced ecosystem is threatened by too many visitors and colonization by mussels escaped from local producers.

Further west, the tiny port of Vivier-sur-Mer once traded in grain and cider apples from farms and orchards inland.

1. The village of Cherrueix, famous for oysters and sand-yachting.
2. Museum of Miniatures of Louis Ame.
3. The wide flat beaches are ideal for sand yachts.
4. A boat gently working up towards Vivier-sur-Mer.
5 and 7. Chapel of Sainte-Anne on the Duchesse Anne dyke.
6. One of the characteristic kidney-shaped lagoons in the tidal salt marshes west of Mont St Michel. The building on the narrow promontory is a hunting shelter.
8. Oyster farm buildings at the port of Vivier-sur-Mer.
9. Local mussels are renowned for their quality.
10. The flat-bottomed tourist boats are ideal for trips around the bay.

45

1 2	3	4
5	6 8	
	7 9 10	

Saint-Benoît-des-Ondes

1. The traditional fish traps are made with woven fences.
2. A view of Mont-Dol from the west.
3. The nets are set at the point of the V of these local fish traps.
4 and 5. Château Richeux is part of one of the stylish Maisons de Bricourt, and a wonderful place to stay near Cancale.

This amazing corner of the bay is Brittany's largest producer of shellfish. At low tide you can see forests of black stakes in the sand which are covered with the millions of mussels cultivated here. Between Saint-Benoît and Cherrueix, the mussel farms cover almost 300 square kilometres on the fringes of the bay. From Vivier-sur-Mer, flat-bottomed amphibious boats, similar to those used by the oyster farmers, offer excursions at any state of the tide – a fascinating way to explore the bay and its shellfisheries.

At Saint-Benoît-des-Ondes you can also see numerous V-shaped fish traps on the foreshore, similar to those near Granville but more like

hedges than stone walls. The Saint-Benoît traps are made of stakes and brushwood, and the main catches today are plaice, sole and brown shrimps, the famous *crevettes grises* of the area. The rights to these fish traps are passed down through families and date from the 17th century.

A short detour inland brings you to Mont-Dol, another granite outcrop of the same geological period as Mont St Michel and Tombelaine. You can either follow the D155 from Vivier-sur-Mer for about four kilometres, or take the GR34 footpath across the marshes. Either route brings you to the foot of Mont-Dol and a path up the north side to the chapel on the summit. From here, on a clear day, there are wonderful views over the

marshes and the bay back to Mont St Michel. The 19th century French writer, Chateaubriand, was a student in Dol and a walk to the top of Mont-Dol was one of his favourite pastimes.

Granite quarried from Mont-Dol was used to build the dykes and also the railway line to Dol. In 1872, while quarrying was in progress, giant bones were discovered, probably from a mammoth. This turned out to be one of the most important finds from the Paleolithic era, about 70,000 BC.

Dol-de-Bretagne, just south of Mont-Dol, has a maze of narrow cobbled streets with half-timbered houses. The main shopping street is called Grande Rue des Stuarts, as the family from whom the Stuart kings were descended is reputed to

Cancale and Port de la Houle

come from Dol. The cathedral of St Samson looks far too large for the size of the town. In the 6th century it was the seat of one of the first bishops in Brittany, but after the French Revolution Dol was no longer an independent bishopric. The church has some interesting carvings, statues and stained glass. Near Dol you can find one of the largest megaliths in Europe, 9.5 metres high.

The area bounded by the Bay of Mont St Michel to the east, the English Channel to the north and the River Rance to the west is known locally as Clos-Poulet. During the 15th and 16th centuries, sea captains, shipowners and merchants living in St Malo became very wealthy from trade with the Indies, and from privateering. Many decided to build large manor houses in the country, but close enough to St Malo to be able to continue to keep an eye on their business. These delightful estates in the Clos-Poulet are known as *Malouinières*, many of which are now open to the public. At Saint-Méloir-des-Ondes, the country house of Vaulerault has its garden facing the sea and at Terrelabouet, towards Cancale, is the 17th century manor where Surcouf, the famous privateer from St Malo, spent his youth.

Cancale is one of Brittany's most picturesque fishing harbours. Sheltered under Pointe de la Chaîne, with its back to the prevailing winds, Cancale was one of the famous cod ports whose fishermen went off for months each year to Newfoundland and the North Atlantic. During this era the women of Cancale developed a reputation for being brave and resourceful and, as with many fishing communities, they had to run the town and their families while the men were away at sea.

Mention Cancale to a Frenchman and he will think of oysters, assuming, of course, that he's not thinking about them already. Cancale specialises in these most succulent and aristocratic of shellfish, and the colourful waterfront is lined with bistros and restaurants offering tantalising menus of *fruits de mer* and *dégustation d'huîtres*. You can also buy oysters and mussels from stalls on the quay – little light takeaways, Breton-style.

1. **Pointe du Grouin with Cancale and Port de la Houle in the foreground. To the right is Pointe de la Chaîne and the Rimains islands.**
2. **The quayside at Port de la Houle has a row of tempting restaurant terraces.**
3. **Cancale oysters are reputed to be the best in France.**
4. **A typical restaurant on the quay at Cancale.**
5. **Oyster farmers busy amongst the *parcs* at low water.**

1		
2		5
3	4	

Cancale and Port de la Houle

1. The north mole of Cancale harbour at low water.
2. The late Éric Tabarly loved to helm *La Cancalaise*.
3. The port of la Houle, with its boats and colourful houses, is a favourite subject for artists.
4. A villa amongst the trees on the cliffs near Cancale.
5. Local fishermen built the Épi (breakwater).
6. An amphibious oyster barge.
7. Lunch is a serious business at Château

Richeux in the Restaurant le Coquillage, where Olivier Roellinger is one of the most respected chefs in Brittany.
8. The Museum of Folk Art and Traditions.

Two stages of oyster cultivation are carried out at Cancale – maturing and cleaning. The vast acres of beds well out in the bay are used for maturing, and the oysters stay out here on their tidal racks for two years in mesh sacks, known as *poches*. The strong currents of cool water through the Bay of Mont St Michel create ideal conditions for the young molluscs to flourish, and teams of cultivators go out regularly in their specially designed flat-bottomed boats to turn the *poches*

at low water. Later, the maturing oysters are moved to the cleaning *parcs* (or *dégorgeoirs*) just below Cancale harbour, where they gradually flush themselves with mud-free water. The mud is cleaned off the shells by passing the oysters along a conveyor through jets of water.

It's a long patient process, but then eating shellfish is a serious business in France. Some of the best oysters from the Bay of Mont St Michel are usually four or five years old when they appear on your plate.

Cancale is a charming seaside town with a very traditional atmosphere and it's always pleasant to wander round the harbour and watch the oyster boats in action. There's an enticing choice of restaurants on the quayside and Le

Continental, on Quai Thomas, is a long-established favourite for a generous *Plateau de fruits de mer*.

A delightful coastal footpath runs from Cancale out to Pointe du Grouin. Following this route you come first to Pointe de la Chaîne where the tiny Rimains islands extend seawards. As with many small ports, Cancale suffered attacks from enemy fleets over the years – the Spanish, Portuguese and English all had a go at various times. There's a local story that in the wall of Cancale's presbytery you can see a cannonball that was fired towards the town by English ships in 1779. In the late 1700s, a fort was built on the largest Rimain island, now a secluded private residence.

The next bay you reach is Port-Pican, which has plenty of mooring

1	2	3
4	5	7	8
	6		

1. Pointe du Grouin and the popular anchorages of Port-Mer and Port-Pican.
2. Castel de Barbe Brûlée overlooks the bay of Port-Mer.
3. The long road out to the Semaphore on Pointe du Grouin. From the end of the point, in good weather, you can see the whole Bay of Mont St Michel and the distant outline of the Chausey islands to the north.
4. A stroll along the beach at Port-Mer.
5. You can often see *La Cancalaise* at her mooring in Port-Mer.

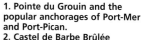

49

1	
2	3
4	5

Cancale to Pointe du Grouin

buoys. Several local boating clubs are based here, with water-skiing, scuba-diving and sailing all very active during the summer. Port-Mer is another popular anchorage, though the bay here is wider and more open to the sea. Castel de Barbe Brûlée – Redbeard's Castle – stands on the cliffs above the bay, now a base for school trips and summer camps. Port-Mer is a pleasant holiday destination with hotels, restaurants and open-air cafés around the beach. A walk out to the tip of Pointe du Grouin gives one of the best views of the Bay of Mont St Michel.

From Pointe du Grouin to the environs of St Malo

East of Pointe du Grouin, Normandy is left behind and Brittany starts in earnest. Imposing cliffs and headlands jut into the Channel, coloured with scattered gorse and broom. Offshore on a summer day, the sea is dotted with hundreds of sails. The unspoilt coast of Clos-Poulet is a paradise of small coves and inlets, and the romantic vibes of Brittany's famous Corsair town seem to hover in the air as you work west towards St Malo.

The coast road from Cancale to Paramé has many places where you can stop and admire the scenery. This is not a route to be rushed, so allow yourself to be diverted out to a headland, down to a beach or simply to sit and gaze out towards the offshore islets and reefs. This approach to St Malo is a perfect introduction to Brittany.

51

1. Enclosed by its stone ramparts, the old town of St Malo seems to have grown out of the granite island on which it perches, and even now is almost completely surrounded by water. It seems unbelievable that the town was virtually razed to the ground at the end of World War II, but the wonderful elegant houses in St Malo's narrow streets are a lasting record of the town's resilience and prosperity.

1

Pointe du Grouin to St Malo

1. Looking east past Anse du Guesclin towards Pointe du Grouin.
2. The west end of Anse du Verger is fringed with dunes.
3. Pointe de la Moulière.
4. The coastal path running past Anse du Verger.
5. The sandy beach at Petit Port between the two headlands on Pointe du Nid.

From Pointe du Grouin to St Malo, the Brittany coast is a succession of sandy bays and rocky outcrops, all fringed by reefs that tend to keep boats a safe distance off. Winds from the west and north-west cause swell to break in plumes of spray on the off-lying rocks. This is a delightful unspoilt coast, with gorse and broom tumbling down the banks of the small valleys and along the cliff edges.

If you can't explore this coast by boat, follow the GR34, the old *Sentier des Douaniers* that winds along the cliffs. In the days of sail this trail was used by excise men and in times of war by lookouts, often young sailors or peasants from neighbouring parishes, keeping a watch for enemy ships – be they privateers or the British navy. Today, this undeveloped coast is a fascinating habitat for wildlife.

From the tip of Pointe du Grouin you see Île des Landes and the narrow channel between the island and the headland. A tail of rocks straggles offshore to the north-east, towards Pierre de Herpin lighthouse and the isolated head of La Fille, which is guarded by a buoy to seaward. To the south-west, a typical North Brittany coastline leads past bays and craggy headlands to St Malo. There are caves in the base of Pointe du Grouin, but anyone exploring them must be careful not to be cut off by the tide. Not far inland, the hamlet of Haut-Bout has a charming chapel where the altar is always decorated with flowers.

The first bay west of Pointe du Grouin is Anse du Verger, where a superb north-facing beach is fringed by dunes. Just in from the west end of the beach is a wild marshy pool, separated from the beach by a bank of rush and marram grass. Overlooking the pool is the little chapel of Notre-Dame-du-Verger. Tradition has it that as the fishing boats rounded Pointe du Grouin on the way to Newfoundland, the sailors always saluted the chapel, asking the Virgin to protect them. Each year, on the morning of the

15th August, mothers, wives and fiancées would go to the chapel to pray and the sailors, hundreds of miles away across the sea, would stop work to light a candle on deck and sing hymns of praise.

Continuing along the coast path you arrive at Petit Port bay, a minute sandy beach in a V between the two headlands of Pointe du Nid. In contrast, the next bay – Plage du Guesclin – is a long sweep of sand with a rocky islet off the east end. In 1757 the Duke of Aiguillon built a fort here to defend the province against English invaders. At low tide you can reach the fortified islet, which now belongs to the Society for the Arts. In the 1960s large

quantities of sand from the bay were used in the construction of the Rance barrage, but now a more ecological view prevails. The dunes are protected with fencing and stonework, with marram grass planted to stabilize the sand.

Beyond Pointe des Grands Nez you reach Anse de la Touesse, sheltered from the prevailing winds by Pointe du Meinga. The east side of this bay has a small, north-facing beach, with a rocky outcrop separating it from a much larger beach with a grand stretch of sand. A narrow lane called Blé-en-Herbe runs from the main coast road down to Anse de la Touesse, passing the manor of Roz Ven once owned by

the French novelist, Colette. She spent many summers here between 1911 and 1926, and the sleepy lane and its *belle plage* inspired her 1923 novel, *Le Blé en Herbe*, a classic love story of long summer holidays. The book was made into a film, directed by Claude Autant-Lara, in 1954. Other writers have been inspired by the scenery around Pointe du Meinga. Much earlier than Colette, Chateaubriand wrote lyrically about

1. Anse de la Touesse and the sheltered summer anchorage on the east side of Pointe du Meinga.
2. Fort du Guesclin is cut off from the mainland at high tide.
3. Manoir de Roz Ven and the beach at Touesse, where Colette spent many summers.
4. The glorious sandy beach at Anse de la Touesse.
5. Cultivated fields come right to the edge of the beach.
6. Fort du Guesclin as the tide falls away.
7 and 8. Gorse and broom along the coastal footpath GR34 as it winds along the cliffs.

Pointe du Grouin to St Malo

**1. With its narrow entrance, Rothéneuf offers a snug retreat for boats that can safely dry out.
2. The long sandy beach of Chevrets, with Rothéneuf inlet in the distance.
3. The malouinière Le Lupin is close to Rothéneuf harbour.
4. Rothéneuf harbour at high water, looking towards the entrance.**

the Breton countryside in *The Martyrs*.

Pointe du Meinga projects into the Channel like a pointing finger. From here round to Pointe de la Varde, the coast has many sandy bays and rocky outcrops. Just west of Meinga, the vast Chevrets beach sweeps round towards Besnard island, which is really a peninsula connected to the mainland by a range of dunes. An old semaphore station stands on the seaward edge of Besnard and there is also a pleasant campsite. The Chevrets sands are fine and white, the sea is an idyllic translucent turquoise and on warm summer days a luxuriant scent of pine hangs in the air.

Immediately to the south, the natural haven at Rothéneuf is a splendid inlet nearly a kilometre wide and extending about one and a half kilometres inland. Rothéneuf is virtually enclosed between the Besnard peninsula and Pointe de Rothéneuf, with only a narrow entry channel for boats. The harbour dries completely at low tide, so any visiting boats must be able to sit on the sand safely, just like the small local boats you find here. In the little village of Rothéneuf, just west of the inlet, is a memorial to Jacques Cartier, the 16th century explorer who claimed Canada for France. Sent by the king to discover a route to the Orient, Cartier discovered the St Lawrence

River. He was born in St Malo and had a country estate, Le Manoir de Limoëlou, near Rothéneuf.

Another feature of Rothéneuf is its amazing collection of carved rocks. The Abbé Fouré was a priest who suffered a stroke which left him deaf. At the age of 54 he retired to Rothéneuf, became something of a hermit and started to carve the rocks around the bay. Between 1893 and 1909 he created over 300 sculptures, some fantastic or grotesque but many identifiable as people. Originally these figures were coloured and had inscriptions explaining who they were, but wind, rain and sun have long obliterated the texts.

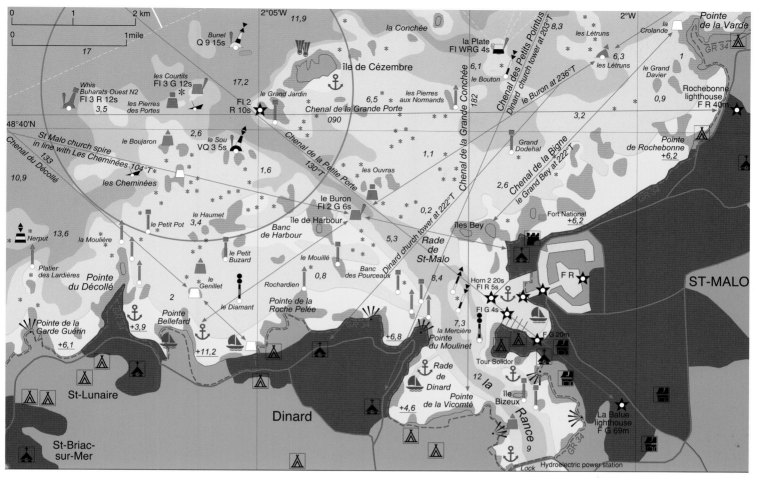

The entrance to the River Rance, with St Malo and Bas-Sablons marina.

Paramé, the resort of St Malo

**1. The sheltered anchorage on the east side of Pointe de la Varde.
2. The Paramé seafront lit at sunset.
3. In westerly winds the beach at Paramé is popular with windsurfers.
4. One of the many good hotels at Paramé.
5. The walled city of St Malo with the port behind. The long breakwater protects the outer harbour and the port entrance from the prevailing winds.**

1	2
3	4
5	

Beyond Pointe de la Varde are St Malo's two main beaches – Minihic and Rochebonne – behind which are the elegant Edwardian villas of Paramé, a sought-after residential neighbourhood of St Malo. Residents of St Malo had started building villas here by the end of the 19th century, and the local population would come out to these beaches on steam trams which ran between Paramé, St Malo and St Servan. Soon entrepreneurs began developing the resort, starting with a promenade along the sea wall between Pointe de Rochebonne and Le Sillon, the spur which links the walled town of St Malo to the mainland. The resort of Paramé was soon drawing as many visitors as

Dinard, on the opposite side of the estuary. It offered many attractions, including horse racing, and there is still a racecourse in St Malo.

The Villa Ker Azur was a centre of literary life in the early 1900s, where the poet Tiercelin entertained many other contemporary poets. The Grand Hôtel de Paramé was the scene of extravagant banquets and was also home to the casino. Paramé became a well-known spa, with all types of seawater and seaweed therapies on offer. This whole spa culture is called *thalassothérapie* in French and is popular in many coastal resorts.

Approaching St Malo from seaward is a magical experience. What appears to be a grey granite island becomes more defined as you get closer, and the steep roofs and

dormer windows gradually appear clearly over the ramparts, with the elegant spire of the cathedral in the centre. The massive breakwater, Môle des Noires, juts out to the charted drying line, protecting the outer harbour from any weight of sea.

The city was founded by a Welsh monk, St Maclou, who arrived in Brittany in the 7th century to convert the local population. The earliest settlement was at Aleth, close to Saint-Servan, but in the 12th century Bishop Jean de Châtillon felt this was vulnerable to attack and moved the community to a rocky outcrop which became an island at high tide and could be more easily defended. It was a proud boast of the city that it had never been conquered, at least until World War II.

The famous ramparts enclosing St Malo were erected and in the early 1400s the castle was built just outside the walls. Some stories suggest this was as much to keep the Malouins in check as to protect them from invaders. The Duchesse Anne was responsible for building the two towers nearest the city walls. Quic-en-Groigne tower now houses St Malo's Hôtel de Ville. The Bidouane Tower, built in the 15th century, is shaped like a horseshoe.

Some of St Malo's more famous sons set off to discover distant lands or embarked on less reputable careers in slave-trading or priva-teering, preying mostly on Dutch and British ships. St Malo became a very prosperous city and brought back wealth for the kings of France. The shipowners and successful captains made substantial fortunes, and during the 16th, 17th and 18th centuries built elegant houses within the ramparts of the city. They also bought country estates and built beautiful manor houses, called *malouinières*, to which they could escape from the city and ultimately retire. For four years at the end of the 16th century, St Malo pro-claimed itself a republic when the citizens refused an alliance with Henri IV.

During one attack by British ships in 1693, a ship packed with explosives was launched towards the walls in an attempt to breach them, but the assault was unsuc-cessful. In the first half of the 18th century, St Malo's ramparts were modified and enlarged four times under the management of Siméon de Garengeau, one of Vauban's engineers. An unusual fact about the walls is that they have no foundations, but simply rest on the natural rock on which the city is built. Careful interlocking, immense thick-ness and the sheer weight of stone have held the walls up for centuries, even withstanding heavy bombard-ment from the American 8th army during the Liberation in 1944. The city has seven rather grand gates. Today most visitors enter through Porte St-Vincent which is close to the castle, or the Grande Porte, halfway along the landward side of the ramparts. There are three gates on the seaward side from where you can reach some of St Malo's beaches.

St Malo, the walled city

1. St Malo *intra-muros* and the inner Vauban marina, a snug mooring place for visiting yachts.
2. Tourists on the ramparts feeding the gulls.
3 & 6. Relaxing on the ramparts.
4. Pilings at the foot of the ramparts are to protect the foundations against erosion by the sea.
5. You can walk round the whole *intra-muros* along the ramparts, which was originally the watchman's path.

	1		
2	3	4	5
		6	

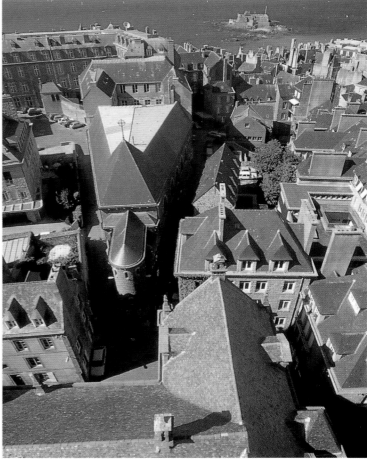

St Malo, the walled city

1. The strikingly shaped castle at St Malo is just outside the walled city.
2. Looking down into the narrow streets of the walled city.
3. The tower at the top of the keep in the St Malo castle. This now houses the city museum (Musée d'Histoire de la Ville et du Pays Malouin).
4. The Town Hall façade.
5. The Mill Tower is attributed to the duchesse Anne who, at the beginning of the 16th century, reinforced the castle's defences with three new towers.

During the Vendée uprising after the French Revolution, and throughout later attempts by the Royalists to regain power in France, St Malo remained staunchly republican. England's support for the French aristocracy and its émigrés simply strengthened opposition from the population of St Malo, because of the long history of battles with the British navy.

When privateering was out lawed in the 19th century, St Malo's prosperity began to decline. The citizens had to find other ways to make their livelihoods from the sea, and St Malo became one of the important cod-fishing ports whose fishermen went off to Newfoundland for six or eight months every year. Shipbuilding and a commercial port also developed.

Believing that a large number of German troops were holding out here, the American army rained shells onto the walled town in August 1944. Incendiary devices were also used and over three-quarters of the old buildings were totally destroyed and the others damaged. The cathedral spire had earlier been shelled by a German submarine.

Immediately after World War II, the mayor of St Malo, Guy la Chambre, oversaw a faithful reconstruction of the old city. Many visitors today have no idea the buildings they are visiting and admiring are not original.

St Malo is one of the most popular tourist locations in France and visitors usually start with a stroll around the ramparts, a distance of about two kilometres. From their vantage you can look out to sea over the various forts in the estuary, along the sandy beaches, across the basins of the harbour, down into the narrow streets or maybe glimpse into some of the windows that are level with the ramparts. At any time of day this is a delightful introduction to the intra-muros. Around the ramparts you can see statues of

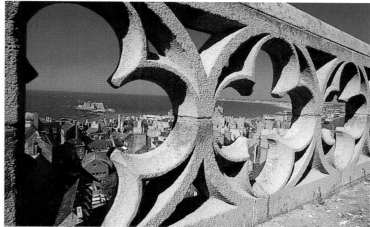

some of the city's most famous inhabitants. Duguay-Trouin and Surcouf were both successful corsairs, some might call them pirates, and the great explorer Jacques Cartier stands forever gazing over the Rance and the port.

Porte Saint-Vincent is now the main entrance to the city. It was built in 1708 to ease the access of carriages. The tourist office is located here and this is where you can join a guided walk of the city. Entering through the gate you come into Place Chateaubriand, named after one of St Malo's illustrious sons, lined with cafés and restaurants where you can sit over a coffee or a beer and absorb the atmosphere.

The cathedral of St Vincent is

near the centre of the old town and its stained glass windows wonderfully illuminate the interior on a sunny day. You can also climb up the tower to a viewing platform from which there are panoramic views over St Malo and across the bay. In the castle near the east walls, don't miss a visit to the town museum. This absorbing exhibition is in the keep, the earliest part of the castle to be built, which was later surrounded by the courtyard and four towers you can see today. The keep (Le Grand Donjon) was damaged in 1944 but restored to its original plan after the war.

St Malo, the walled city

59

1. The courtyard of La Houssaye, a hint of the Middle Ages within the walls of St Malo.
2. From the tower of the cathedral you can savour panoramic views towards Pointe de la Varde and the Fort National.
3. Place Chateaubriand is lined with cafés.
4. St Malo's main beach, La Grande Plage, with Fort National in the distance.
5. Bon Secours beach is close under the ramparts and has a seawater swimming pool.

The port of St Malo

1. The port of St Malo with its commercial docks and marinas, the entrance to the River Rance and the town of Dinard in the distance.
2. The sheltered Vauban basin is at the foot of the ramparts.
3. A ship in St Malo's dry dock.
4 and 5. Timber and granite are important cargoes that come into St Malo.

1
2	3	4	5

The sturdy Môle des Noires is 180 metres long and protects the outer harbour and dock approaches from the worst of the weather. St Malo welcomes yachtsmen into either Port des Bas-Sablons, entered over a sill just before the lock, or to the sheltered pontoons in Bassin Vauban, right under the city ramparts. The inner basin has been the scene of many nautical festivals, including the Tall Ships Race and transatlantic races such as the Route du Rhum. These events attract thousands of spectators keen to watch the preparations and catch a glimpse of famous racing yachtsmen.

From Quai de Dinan in the outer harbour, under the ramparts near Port de Dinan, ferries leave to cross the estuary to Dinard, and you can also start a boat trip around the bay or up the River Rance. From the Gare Maritime, ferries shuttle regularly to England and the Channel Islands. St Malo is one of the busiest ferry ports in Brittany.

The dramatic range of tide in the Bay of St Malo meant the original settlement was an island at high water. Over the centuries quays were built around the city and eventually, to ensure deepwater berths for ships, locks were built at the entrance to the docks. The first lock gives access to Bassin Vauban and then the fishing port is reached through a swing bridge in Bassin Bouvet. The St Malo fishing fleet has both deep-sea and inshore trawlers, as well as local boats gathering shellfish. The commercial port is in Bassin Jacques-Cartier and Bassin Duguay-Trouin. Typical cargoes shipped through St Malo are timber, fertilizer and granite, but many other types of goods are carried, including agricultural produce.

To maintain its reputation of impregnability, St Malo had to upgrade its defences as the artillery capabilities of its enemies developed. After several serious attacks by the British navy, Vauban drew up a plan for a double layer of defensive forts, some out to sea, with smaller forts and watchtowers on land. The fortress at Pointe de la Varde was built in 1758 on the site of an older battery and this became the outer limit of St Malo's fortifications. The Fort National, originally called Fort Royal, can be reached by foot at low water and is open to the public. Under the direction of Siméon de Garangeau it was completed in 1689 on a rocky islet just off the coast. There had previously been a

type of early light signal maintained here as a guide to sailing ships. The fort was built of granite from Chausey and was defended by about 60 gunners. It was particularly active during the defence of St Malo against the Anglo-Dutch forces in 1693. The final tragedy to take place in the fort was in August 1944 when citizens of St Malo were held in there by the Germans and the fort was shelled by the American army.

Fort Petit-Bé was built between 1689 and 1693 as part of the same plan and was intended to protect the entrance to the Rance. Its walls were constructed in such a way that defenders had a 360° firing range. The original plans included a drawbridge but this was never built.

You can walk out to the fort at low tide from Bon Secours beach.

Fort de la Conchée is two miles offshore and Vauban regarded it as the bridgehead of the defences. Built on Petite Conchée rock, its curved walls drop straight into the sea, making the fort look like a ship. Building la Conchée was particularly difficult because of its position and in 1693 the English captured the

1. The inner approaches to St Malo at half-tide. Petit-Bé is in the foreground, and at this stage of the ebb Grand-Bé and Fort National can be reached by foot.

2. The fortress on Pointe de la Varde, north-east of St Malo. The battery was modernised in 1898 and fortified by the German army during World War II. It is now a listed site.
3. The Fort National was the centrepiece of St Malo's defences. It was built by Siméon de Garangeau in 1689 and heavily armed. Over the centuries it has served the city well, particularly during the Anglo-Dutch attack in 1693.

1	
2	3

The forts of St Malo

1. Île Cézembre, on the right, has a sandy beach on its south side. It was a retreat for monks from St Malo during the Middle Ages. The lighthouse of Grand-Jardin is on the edge of the rocks, guarding the main channel into St Malo.
2. Fort La Conchée was St Malo's outer defence. It is now a listed historical monument.
3. The slipway on Île Cézembre.
4. The distinctively shaped Fort Petit-Bé, at the mouth of the Rance.
5. Île Harbour.

fort and took the labourers prisoner. Vauban insisted on its completion and by 1695 the battery based there prevented the English ships getting close enough to bombard St Malo. Most of its buildings have now been destroyed but an association has been formed which hopes to restore Fort de la Conchée to its former glory.

Another fort was built in the St Malo approaches on Île Cézembre and its batteries were part of the outer defences of the city. All trace of these buildings seems to have been destroyed during the Second World War. You can visit the island on one of the boat trips which explore the bay and leave from St Malo's Quai de Dinan or the Clair de Lune Promenade at Dinard.

Harbour island, to the west of the entrance and north of Dinard, was also fortified by Garangeau. The fort had a steep cliff on the landward side but was vulnerable to an enemy landing from seaward, so a lower wall following the island's contours was also built. The fortifications on Harbour island are now a historical monument, but they are privately owned so not accessible to the public.

Grand-Bé island had a small fort, but Vauban's plans for it to be enlarged were never carried through. The fortifications were almost completely destroyed during World War II. Grand-Bé is probably better known, particularly in France, as the burial place of the writer François-René de Chateaubriand who was buried there on 18th July 1848. His tomb was restored after the war.

Further along the coast from St Malo, Fort du Guesclin, the batteries at Verger, Garde-Guérin, Île du Perron, Île des Hébihens and Fort la Latte were all part of Vauban's grand defensive plan of the Emerald Coast, which proved highly effective.

The strategic position of the Aleth peninsula at the mouth of the Rance made it an ideal site for a fort. In the late 17th century Vauban included the location in his defence plans, but it wasn't until 1758, after several successful incursions by English troops, that the Aleth fort was completed. During World War II the occupying German forces reinforced this stronghold and extended the underground rooms and passages to make it the centre of their fortress St Malo. An anti-aircraft emplacement, artillery battery and command headquarters were all based at Aleth and the whole peninsula was heavily fortified. A memorial to World War II is now housed in the anti-aircraft blockhouse.

The history of the Aleth peninsula goes back to pre-Christian times. It was the capital of an early Gaulish tribe, the Coriosolites, and later a Gallo-Roman fort was built there. Aleth was attacked many times by Norman invaders and in the Middle Ages the monastic settlement moved to the island which is now St Malo, as this was easier to defend. Archaeological digs have found evidence of a village of wooden huts and an ancient port in Solidor bay.

The peninsula now has a delightfully rural campsite with some of the most beautiful views of the estuary, St Malo itself, across to Dinard and up to the mouth of the River Rance. A footpath runs right around the peninsula – La Corniche d'Aleth – from which you can see the marina of Bas-Sablons. Opposite St Servan beach, a seawater pool is retained by a dam at the head of the marina inlet. A sill at the marina entrance lets yachts come and go except near low water.

Saint-Servan is now technically part of St Malo but feels quite independent and less geared to tourism. The town has a full range of shops and a regular outdoor market. There are pretty villas, parks and gardens to explore, and in the centre the church of Sainte-Croix. South of the Aleth peninsula are two bays, Port St Père and Port Solidor, divided by a short rocky spur on which stands the Solidor tower. The original keep was built between

1. The Aleth peninsula with the Bas-Sablons marina behind and St Malo in the distance. The Tour Solidor is in the foreground with the town of Saint-Servan on the right.

1

Saint-Servan and Aleth

1. Evening light on the Solidor tower.
2. Bouvet Place in the centre of Saint-Servan.
3. The Rosais cemetery in Saint-Servan.
4. Tour Solidor is now home to the Cape Horners museum.
5. Notre-Dame-Dominatrice, the dramatic statue on the top of la Vierge de Bizeux rock, between Saint-Servan and Pointe de la Vicomté.

1369 and 1382 and derives its name from the Styridor rock which forms its foundation. Duc Jean IV de Bretagne ordered its construction to protect the entrance of the Rance when St Malo rebelled against his authority. La Tour Solidor is actually made up of three towers linked by a central square, with battlements 27 metres above the sea. When military developments made the tower redundant, it became a prison and today houses the museum of Cape Horners.

This exhibition evokes the history of countless tall ships and clippers that sailed round Cape Horn from the time of Sir Francis Drake through Captain Cooke right up to the 19th century. This adventure story of trade and exploration is traced through models, maps, old photographs, nautical memorabilia, ships in bottles and, of course, a very large albatross. The breathtaking view from the top of Tour Solidor takes in the coast around Dinard and the estuary up to the Rance barrage. At the base of the tower, a cross commemorates Jacques Cartier's departure from here on his second voyage to Canada in 1535.

Local boats moor in both Port St Père and Port Solidor, sitting in the mud at low water. Visiting yachts can sometimes find a vacant mooring buoy opposite the beach. The St Servan riverfront has several restaurants and cafés along the quay, and there are more up in the main part of town.

Dinard, a resort of the Bell Époque

Just across the estuary from St Malo, Dinard is the most famous resort of the Emerald Coast. Before it was made popular by English visitors in the mid 19th century, there was just a small fishing village here called St Énogat, which faced out towards the Channel. Some of the local men would have joined the cod-fishing voyages to Newfoundland, and some just fished locally and acted as ferrymen to take passengers across to St Malo. A few of the successful Malouin shipowners built houses here in the 17th and 18th centuries, but the town really developed during the Belle Époque.

In the 1850s a few English families who lived on the Continent started to spend their summers in Dinard and the first villa to be built, called St Catherine, was for the Faber family. Other English and American families, who had previously taken holidays in Dinan or Avranches, were then drawn to the area with its mild climate and two distinct aspects, one out to sea and a softer outlook onto the river. Paul Féart, mayor of the town in the 1860s, started to promote Dinard as a resort. Ten years later, with the arrival of the Lebanese Count Rochaïd Dahdah, property development started to boom.

In 1887 the railway reached Dinard, making travel easier and transforming the town into the most elegant resort in France. At the turn of the 20th century the upper classes, and even royalty, were attracted to Dinard. Luxurious hotels were opened and in 1910 the first casino was built. By 1928 the town had four casinos, promenades and public gardens were built and its prosperity continued until World War II.

Several of the villas from the Belle Époque can still be seen today, particularly around Plage de Saint-

1. Pointe du Moulinet with its elegant villas and Dinard in the background.
2. Overlooking Prieuré bay is Dinard's aquarium and Museum of the Sea. The museum describes the polar expeditions of Commander Charcot and also houses a maritime laboratory.
3. Château de la Vicomté.
4. Pointe du Moulinet.
5. A typical Dinard villa of the Belle Époque, with its ornate turrets, bay windows, traditional shutters and spacious verandas.
6. The villas on Pointe de la Malouine are built right to the edge of the beach.

Dinard, a resort of the Belle Époque

1. Dinard and the bay at half-tide. The deeper water can be seen in the approach channel and around the marina pontoons.
2. Dinard marina at high tide.
3. The Dinard golf course is actually at St Briac-sur-Mer, between Pointe de la Garde-Guérin and Pointe de la Haye. This is the second oldest golf course in France.

4. Saint-Énogat beach.
5. The orientation table up on Pointe du Moulinet.

6. The swimming pool on Plage de l'Écluse is simply a dam at the top of the beach.

Énogat, Pointe de la Malouine and Pointe du Moulinet. To explore the area you can follow the GR34 footpath from the west end of the Rance barrage right round to Plage de Saint-Énogat. This route is a delightful mix of wooded paths, sandy beaches and town promenades. You round Pointe de la Vicomté along a rocky path before coming down to the beach at Prieuré Bay. Further on you reach the popular Promenade du Clair de Lune which passes the port with its small marina. From here you can catch a ferry across to St Malo.

The route continues along the old *Sentier des Douaniers* round Pointe du Moulinet, past Plage de l'Écluse and on to Pointe de la Malouine before reaching Plage de Saint-Énogat. Walking back through the town outskirts to the centre of Dinard, you can see many villas that have been family holiday homes for generations. For most of the year the shutters are closed, but in July and August these fine old houses come to life, with beach towels on the verandas and the chatter of families on holiday.

	1	
2	4	5
3		6

Exploring the Rance

The River Rance rises on the moorlands in the Côtes-d'Armor, about 100 kilometres from the sea. The young river joins the Canal d'Ille-et-Rance and then passes under the ramparts of Dinan, where it starts to widen gently as far as the lock at Châtelier. The main estuary then develops into a series of creeks and muddy inlets, gently linking the countryside to the sea. This section down to the barrage is semi-tidal, and the rural atmosphere seems a world away from wind and waves.

Above the barrage the valley is rural but not wild or remote. Sleepy hamlets, neat farms and ancient woods placidly enclose a very civilised navigable corridor steeped in that unique French blend of privilege and equality. There are delightful country cottages and charming houses that have been owned by the same families for generations. Locals and visitors have easy access to the river, which has plenty of public slips and landings where anyone can launch a small boat and savour all that the Rance has to offer.

67

1. The narrowest part of the Rance estuary just below Le Châtelier lock.
2. The elegant Malouinière du Montmarin depicted in an 18th century painting.

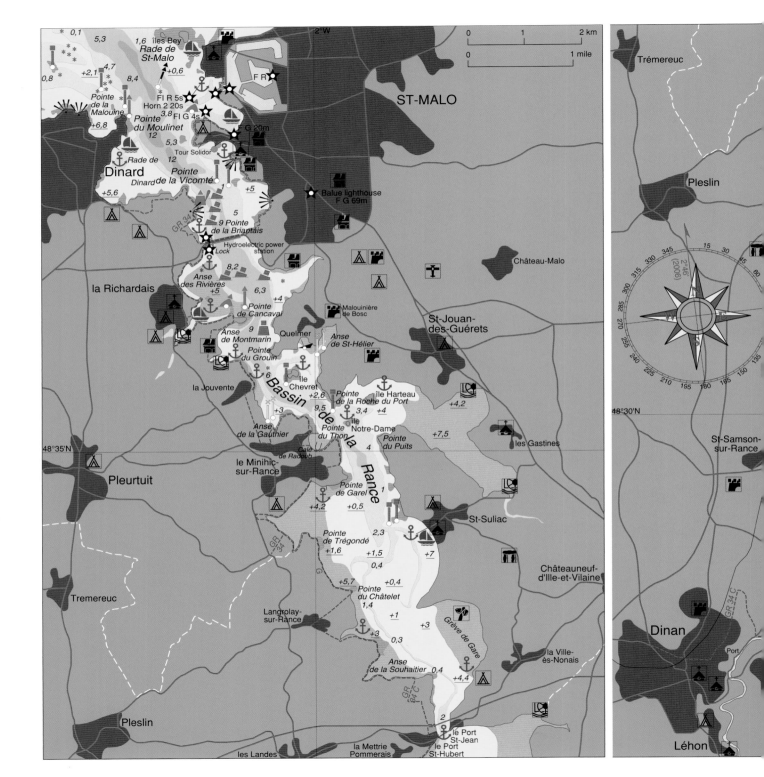

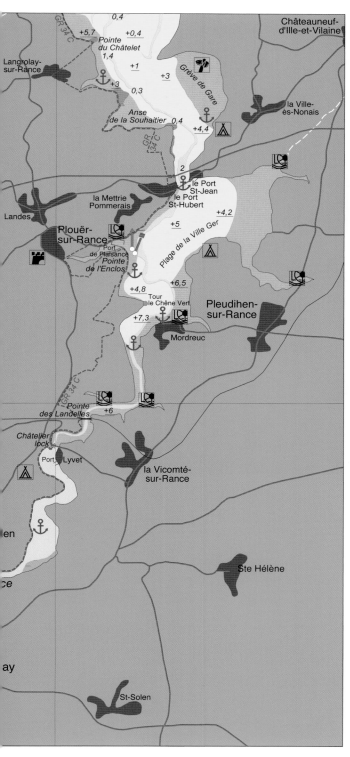

Châteauneuf-
d'Ille-et-Vilaine

0,4
+5,7
Pointe
du Châtelet
1,4
+1
+3
0,3
Langrolay-
sur-Rance
+3
Grève de Gare
Anse
de la Souhaitier 0,4
la Ville-
ès-Nonais
+4,4
2
le Port
St-Jean
le Port
St-Hubert
la Mettrie
Pommerais
+4,2
Landes
+5
Plage de la Ville Ger
Plouër-
sur-Rance
Port
de Plaisance
Pointe
de l'Enclos
+6,5
+4,8
Tour
le Chêne Vert
Pleudihen-
sur-Rance
+7,3
Mordreuc
Pointe
des Landelles
+6
Châtelier
lock
Port Lyvet
la Vicomté-
sur-Rance
Ste Hélène
St-Solen

The tide mills of the Rance

69

There used to be many tidal mills on the Rance. The Beauchet mill, at the head of Goutte bay, was working until the beginning of World War II. The flood tide would fill the millpond, and then water was released on the ebb to turn the paddle wheel. Millers often owned a windmill as well, to cover the period of neap tides.
1. The Marelle mill.
2. The Beauzais mill.

The Rance Barrage

1. The mouth of the Rance looking seaward, with the power station barrage in the foreground and St Malo and Dinard in the distance. You can clearly see the wash as the tide passes through the turbines. There is a lock 65m long and 13m wide at the west end near Pointe de la Brebis, to allow boats free passage. The road linking St Malo and Dinard passes along the top of the barrage, with a lifting bridge over the lock to allow masted boats to enter the upper Rance. The approaches to the barrage are well buoyed to keep boats away from the turbines.

The 750 metre hydroelectric barrage across the Rance carries the road linking St Malo to Dinard between Pointe de la Briantais on the east side and Pointe de la Brebis on the west. The idea of using the tide to generate electricity had been considered since the 1920s but work on the power station didn't start until 1961. The Rance estuary was chosen for this project because of its massive tidal range, up to 14 metres on a big spring tide. Above the barrage the natural river reservoir has a capacity of 185 million cubic metres, which represents a considerable generating potential.

The power station itself was built by 1963 but the whole barrage project took another three years to complete. General de Gaulle presided at the opening ceremony on 26th of November 1966. This was the first tidal hydroelectric scheme in the world. The Rance turbines operate on both the flood tide and the ebb tide and the timing is computer controlled. This means that the tides above the barrage are out of phase with the natural tide and are compressed into a shorter period, three or four hours rather than six.

The power station has 24 turbines of 10 megawatts each and is the major electricity generator in Brittany.

The creation of the barrage has changed the ecosystem of the river. There is now a gradual build-up of mud and silt above the barrage, as the valley is no longer scoured by the tide. Fish species have also changed. Because larger, slower-moving species cannot pass the turbines, plaice and sand eels are no longer found above the barrage but bass and cuttlefish have been. The power station itself has now become a tourist attraction and visitors also gather to watch boats passing through the lock.

Manor houses of the Rance and Clos-Poulet

The concept and name of *malouinière* comes from the late 1500s, pre-dating the era of the great ship-owners by about a hundred years. These early summer homes were built quite close to St Malo. Two of the best-known examples are Limoëlou, owned by the explorer Jacques Cartier, and the manor at Gué belonging to the privateer Duguay-Trouin. By the end of the 17th century, the shipowners made wealthy by foreign trade started to build these gentlemen's residences in the Malouin countryside, where they could retreat and relax.

Throughout Clos-Poulet and along each bank of the Rance, there are over 100 *malouinières* of different styles and sizes. Invariably they were built in secluded places and often protected by a discreet garden or a boundary wall. Interestingly, only three *malouinières* have their frontages and gardens towards the sea, so most owners were seeking a more rural landscape away from their maritime work.

The architecture of most *malouinières* is quite sober and almost military in style. The facades tend to be symmetrical, an impression reinforced by the roof-lines which often have matching dormer windows and paired chimneys at each end of the house. Inside, however, the furnishings and decor were sumptuous. The ship-owners imported exotic woods and materials from distant lands, such as fine Cuban mahogany for furniture, panelling and floors, marble from Venice for fireplaces, hides from Russia for upholstery or decorative tiles from Delft.

By the 18th century, the second wave of *malouinières* turned out to be even more splendid. Many of these later houses became their owner's main residence, rather than just a summer home. As plots within the city became more expensive and the shipowners and merchants became richer from trade with Spain, they spared no expense on their country estates. Some of the *malouinières* were more like castles than manor houses. Although these properties

1. The *malouinière* Lupin at Saint-Coulomb is one of only three built facing the sea.
2. A classic circular dovecote is often found in the grounds of a *malouinière*.
3 and 4. The *malouinière* Mettrie-aux-Louëts was built in 1725.

1	2
3	4

Manor houses of the Rance and Clos-Poulet

72

1. The tide mill at La Richardais.
2. The grounds of la Fosse-Hingant *malouinière* go down to the Sainte Suzanne lake, close to St Coulomb.
3. Basse-Fleurie is on the right bank of the Rance, just above the barrage.
4. The calm French gardens at Montmarin come right down to the shore of the Rance.

| 1 | 3 |
| 2 | 4 |

were very beautiful, they didn't compare with the opulent summer homes built by the shipowners of Nantes or Parisian courtiers. Visitors to the Rance tended to be slightly snobbish, referring to the *malouinières* as simply traders' country homes.

From a boat on the Rance you can see some of the *malouinières* whose grounds come down to the shore. On the west side, close to La Richardais, is the Domaine of Montmarin where the gardens are regularly open to the public. Although the lawns sweep right down to the shoreline it's the sort of place you spot only briefly before the clever angles of the gardens

close off this tantalising glimpse of gracious living. Montmarin was built in 1760 by a Monsieur Aaron Magon in the elegant style of Louis XV. The roof of Montmarin is reminiscent of the shape of an upturned boat and from the terraced gardens you can watch yachts sailing up the river.

After the death of Monsieur Magon his widow sold Montmarin in 1782, to a shipbuilder from Saint-Servan, Benjamin Dubois, who created a port in the creek just upstream from the house. This busy dock built ships which started running regularly between France and New York. An attempt was made during the French Revolution

for the state to take over this property, but the agreement was never completed and the family stayed at Montmarin. When ship-building declined in the early 1800s a dam was built across the shipyard creek and a tide mill was built which was working until the start of the Great War.

Set in parkland overlooking the barrage, Château Briantais is the former home of Guy La Chambre, the mayor of St Malo who oversaw the reconstruction of the city after 1944. The grounds and woodlands cover the whole headland from Vau Garni in the north to Troctin bay in the south. The park was laid out in the English style by Denis and Eugène Bühler using native trees, giving glorious open views up the Rance valley and downstream to Solidor bay. The property is now owned by the diocese and used for cultural events. It is open to the public on Saturday and Sunday afternoons all year round.

Anse de Troctin is the first river bay upstream from the barrage. Even before the barrage was built, this bay was out of the main tidal currents and a thick layer of mud settled here. Because of this, Troctin was chosen by the master carpenters of the Rance shipyards as the place to season timber. Oak, ash or elm that would later be used to make keels, frames, ribs and stems was left in the salty mud for two years, a treatment that protected the wood against rot and parasites.

At the tip of the next headland is the slipway at La Passagère, from which a ferry used to cross the river to the opposite slip at Jouvente. On the high ground above La Passagère is the family home of Commander Charcot, the polar explorer, who lived there to relax and recuperate between expeditions. The location also let him follow the progress of the construction of his next vessel

1. Looking seaward down the Rance, with Pointe de Garel in the left foreground sheltering the at the shipyard on the opposite bank at La Landriais.

Up into the bay past La Passagère, and protected by Chevret island, you will find one of the saddest sights on the Rance, a boat graveyard. At the head of the creek in varying stages of decay, the last remains of old wooden hulls poke up from the mud. Gradually nature reclaims these skeletons but you can still almost feel a hint of the sea and ghostly voyages in the atmosphere surrounding them.

Just past the barrage lock on the

La Richardais

anchorage at Minihic-sur-Rance. The bay opening to the right is La Goutte and the barrage can just be seen in the distance.
2. High water at La Richardais launching slip.
3. La Briantais *malouinière* is now used for cultural events.
4. The narrow inlet at La Richardais, where the tide mill, its dam and millpond have all been carefully preserved.
5. La Richardais and its slip almost completely dry at low tide.

1		
2	4	5
3		

The barrage to Pointe du Crapaud

1. La Landriais and its boatyard at high water.
2. La Passagère slip and the family home of Commander Charcot.
3, 4 and 8. La Landriais.
5. The home of Commander Charcot – doctor, sailor and Arctic explorer.
6. An abandoned trawler gently rotting away in a quiet corner of the Rance.
7. The remains of the graving dock for the old

1	2

3	4	5	6

7	8	9

Lemarchand shipyard, which was in business at La Landriais in the early 1900s.

9. The anchorage behind La Passagère is sheltered by Île Chevret Island.

west bank, a secluded path follows the shoreline of the river, winding in and out of the bays and creeks. At La Richardais you can see Optimists from the sailing school out on the river, the next generation of yachtsmen learning their craft. Along the narrow inlet above the village you pass the old tide mill with its dam and millpond. The path continues round Pointe de Cancaval and skirts behind the *malouinière* of Montmarin before coming down to the slip at La Jouvente. This is one

of the most interesting walks along the Rance valley, with delightful views of the river. From here you can see the current pouring over the rocks at the end of the point, and boats tucking in close to keep inside the buoyed channel to the lock. In the bay at La Landriais, opposite Île Notre-Dame, a busy local boatyard has a long slipway where yachts are hauled out onto dry land. Here you can see the remains of a graving dock for the old Lemarchand shipyard. Built in 1910, the dock was 45m long and 10m wide, and worked on the principle of a lock. At high water a boat would enter the dock and be carefully secured. Once the tide had fallen away, the end doors were

closed and the boat remained high and dry throughout its refit. It was at the Lemarchand yard that Commander Charcot's ship was built and refitted for polar expeditions.

The GR34 path follows the west shore of the Rance, winding round the headlands and in and out of all the creeks and bays as far as Dinan. On the way you can make charming detours into villages such as Minihic-sur-Rance or Plouër-sur-Rance.

The Bay of La Goutte cuts well inland on the east side of the Rance, and its upper reaches were once used as salt pans with the help of salt workers from Guérande. This vast muddy bay is now a reserve for migratory birds and you often see herons searching the mudflats. At the head of the bay is the old Beauchet tide mill, where the mill-pond has been converted into a fish farm.

On the river side of the peninsula, St Suliac is possibly the most picturesque Rance village, with its bay stretching round from Pointe de Grainfollet to Pointe du Mont Gareau. The traditional occupation of the village fishermen was catching sand eels. From the long St Suliac landing slip, slate-roofed houses climb up towards the church with its high square bell-tower. This 13th century fortified tower has an octagonal tower above it and then a slate spire. The church is unusual in Ille-et-Vilaine, being enclosed by stone walls having two beautiful 13th century gateways. The narrow streets of St Suliac are a joy to wander.

The anchorage lies opposite the long slipway, which is necessary at low tide because the foreshore dries out a long way and becomes very muddy. Visiting yachts can anchor outside the local moorings and the downstream end of the bight has the deepest water. Small local fishing boats, called chippes and rather like dories, used to be common at St Suliac and were built to the design of Lemarchand. These handy craft were used to catch sand eels and could be easily rowed or sailed around sandbanks to lay the nets which were then hauled at low water.

At Grainfollet you can see a stone shrine to the Virgin Mary. This was built by sailors from the village on their return from cod-fishing off Newfoundland in the 1890s. The fishermen had vowed they would build a shrine here if no one died during their hazardous voyage. Because their prayers were granted, they built this sanctuary on coming safely home and now a Pardon takes place on 15th August each year.

1. The long St Suliac landing slip at low tide.
2. The fortified church at St Suliac, surrounded by the slate roofs of the village.
3. The anchorage at St Suliac.
4. Locally built dories, similar to those used on the banks off Newfoundland, are popular boats on the river.
5. A replica local fishing boat, a *chippe*, alongside the slipway at St Suliac.
6. A typical cottage in St Suliac.
7. The shrine to the Virgin Mary on the headland at Grainfollet.

St Suliac to Port St Jean

**1. The Rance near low water with the village of Mordreuc in the foreground. You can just make out the narrow gap between Port St Jean, on the right bank, and Port St Hubert on the left.
2. Pointe de Garel, which shelters the anchorage at Minihic.
3. The Beauchet tide mill at the head of La Goutte.
4. The chapel of Sainte-Anne in the hamlet of Saint-Buc.
5. The decorated crucifix in the church at Minihic-sur-Rance.
6. At low water the strange mosaic-like remains of the Viking camp below**

1	2
3	4 5	6

Mont Gareau can be seen – here you can just make out the stone foundations.

Above St Suliac, the Rance flows more gently, penetrating deeper inland up the small valleys and creeks. At Minihic, on the west bank, the mudflats and marshes extend as far as the quarries. The parishioners of Minihic-sur-Rance built their church in 1926 but it was damaged in the bombardments of 1944 and subsequently needed major restoration work. In the village you might be surprised to see a wooden Calvary where the cross is replaced with an anchor, emphasising the village's links with the sea.

Mont Gareau, on the east shore, is the highest point in the area at 73 metres. From the summit there's a wonderful panorama of the Rance valley and, on a clear day, you can count up to 32 church towers. Excavating the muddy river bed at Ville-ès-Nonais, archaeologists have identified the foundations of a Viking camp, Gardaine, which was an active port and settlement until the Vikings retreated to Normandy in the early 10th century.

The River Rance has cut a dramatic channel through a granite outcrop between Port St Hubert and Port St Jean. This narrow gap with its high steep banks made it easier to build the bridge for the D366 when it replaced the ferry in 1929. Both the bridge and the lock at Châtelier were bombed in June 1944 and were rebuilt in 1957. A second bridge carrying the main road from Dinan to Dol was completed in 1991 just downstream. This later bridge is an elegant single arch and has been christened the Chateaubriand bridge because it connects the Dinan area, where the writer's family came from, to Clos-Poulet where he spent much of his childhood. At river level on either side you can still see the quays which would have been busy with barge traffic in days gone by. Barges were loaded with firewood at Port St Jean to supply St Malo.

Plouër-sur-Rance

Above the narrows at Port St Hubert, the channel of the Rance becomes very narrow on low spring tides. You enter a world of mudflats and marshes, with wading birds searching the mud for food and flocks of geese flying over the riverside fields. As the river becomes less accessible, nature becomes wilder and houses more isolated. For yachtsmen the tides are less predictable, responding to the demands of the hydroelectric plant down at the barrage. The risks of grounding increase and the crew needs to keep a careful watch on the depth as the helmsman follows the winding fairway upstream.

The shallow creek at Plouër, which has an old tidal mill at its mouth, has been converted into a snug marina. The low rubble dam across the creek that once served the mill was built up to form a sill which covers at high water. Inside the sill, lines of pontoons make a delightful sheltered yacht harbour way out in the country with the village about 20 minutes walk away. The Château de Plouër is just outside the village. Built on the site of a former feudal castle, the existing château was erected in the 17th century.

On the promontory of Pointe du Chêne-Vert, surrounded by trees, Château de Péhou is a late 19th century folly built by Prince Basilevski for his mistress, the dancer and singer Marie Éloy. A fort had been built on this strategic site in early times and the walls from a castle of the Middle Ages were still there. Two towers were added and a theatre created where extravagant musical events were performed. The prince gave both the *domaine* of Chêne-Vert and Château des Vaux Carheil to Marie Éloy. She married the composer and pianist Henri Kowalski and they lived on the Rance until the Great War.

1. The two bridges across the Rance narrows, perfectly reflected in the still waters.
2. The delightful marina at Plouër-sur-Rance, entered through a sill-gate at the upstream end of the retaining wall.
3. The old tidal mill at Plouër-sur-Rance – La Minoterie – has been converted into apartments. The sheltered millpond is now a marina basin.
4. Château de Plouër-sur-Rance, with its beautiful facade, steep slate roofs and traditional dovecote.
5. Peaceful moorings in the upper Rance.

Pleudihen-sur-Rance to Châtelier lock

1. Looking down on Le Chêne-Vert and the Château de Péhou.
2. The old mill at Mordreuc has been converted into a crêperie.
3. The slipway near the marina at Plouër-sur-Rance.

4 and 6. The mudflats and meadows at Bas-Champs. As the tide retreats, artistic curves and swirls are left in the mud.
5. The village of Mordreuc with its landing slip. You can see Pointe du Chêne-Vert in the distance.

1	2	3
	4	
	5	6

Following the path along the banks of the Rance, you are sure to have the chance to sample local cider in a small village bistro or bar close to a landing slip. The Rance valley is as famous for cider as Cancale is for oysters. The cider from Pleudihen-sur-Rance is particularly renowned and you can visit the apple and cider museum at La Ville Hervy, upstream from Mordreuc. The museum has an exhibition on cider orchards, examples of apple presses and other vital tools, a film about cider making and, of course, a chance to sample some cider and enjoy a crêpe before you leave.

Pleudihen-sur-Rance was the home for Rance bargemen whose barges – called *gabares* – transported wood, grain, apples, cider, stone or sand from the country down to St Malo. The barges would settle in the mud at Bas-Champs, a creek just downstream of Pleudihen, or at Mordreuc, regarded as the port for Pleudihen. From the 17th century the bargemen used the surrounding forests to supply firewood to the bakers and inhabitants of St Malo and Saint-Servan.

Before the Rance barrage was constructed, the houses near the quay at Mordreuc used to be flooded on high spring tides. This was also a place where, at low water, it was possible to ford the river. Mordreuc had lime kilns for producing either building lime or fertilizer.

Above Mordreuc, the river narrows and the channel winds from side to side dodging steep mudbanks. These higher reaches have a jungle quality, accentuated by the rustic fish traps at the river's edge. From each of these rickety huts, built on stilts, a large net is swung out over the river on a long pole, lowered to the bottom, and then hauled up using a simple winch. The huts shelter the fishermen from rain and, just as important, protect their pâtés, cheeses and wine. The main purpose of these retreats must surely be a quiet lunch.

The 16th century Moulin de Rochefort stands at the mouth of the tiny Coutance river on the left bank of the Rance. As you continue upstream towards the lock at Châtelier, a more modern building is visible before the railway bridge at Lessart. This tide mill was unusual as it included the mill itself, a bread oven and the baker's house. The impressive viaduct at Lessart carries the railway line between Dol-de-Bretagne and Dinan across the river.

The GR34 footpath crosses the railway line about 90 metres above the river, giving beautiful views of the Rance and the Renaissance-style Châtelier castle. About two kilometres east of the bridge is Bellière castle, the family home of the first wife of Bertrand du Guesclin, a 14th century knight. Du Guesclin was renowned for his tactics in fighting the English during the Hundred Years War.

The last few hundred yards before Châtelier lock are narrow and tortuous, marked by spar beacons rather than buoys. By boat it's best to arrive on the last of the Rance flood or during the high-water stand, creeping up slowly, especially if another boat is coming down. Once past the Châtelier lock, the river changes from maritime to inland, where the tide no longer dictates your movements and the water feels still and calm.

From Pleudihen-sur-Rance to Châtelier lock

1. Looking downstream from Lessart railway bridge.

2. Châtelier lock with the canalized Rance above and the muddy tidal reaches below.

3. Château de Châtelier.
4, 5 and 6. The rustic fish traps at the river's edge on the way up to Châtelier lock.
7. A boat approaching the Châtelier lock between the muddy banks.
8. Boats in Châtelier lock waiting for the water to rise.

1	2	
3	4	7
5	6	8

The canalized Rance

1. Lyvet marina is just above Châtelier lock on the right bank.
2. Above Châtelier, the Ille-et-Rance canal begins. From here a boat can start on an inland journey past Tinténiac and Hédé to Rennes and across Brittany to the Bay of Biscay.
3. Steep cliffs border the Rance at Taden.
4. The towpath is open to cyclists and walkers.
5. Canoes are popular on the canalized Rance.

Immediately above the lock at Châtelier, the river widens out. On the right bank is Port Lyvet marina and opposite are boats on mooring buoys. This is the start of the Canal d'Ille-et-Rance which links the Channel coast through to Rennes and ultimately the Biscay coast via the River Vilaine. When the canal was a busy trade route, Port Lyvet had quays where inland barges would load and discharge cargoes such as cider, grain, potatoes or firewood, which were then taken down the estuary to St Malo. The marina now occupies the quays and

is an attractive place to keep a boat.

The towpath is on the left bank and the GR34 follows the path all the way to Dinan. Walkers have to share the path with cyclists who can enjoy this level route for the seven kilometres up to the town. Below the village of Taden, the river narrows with cliffs on the towpath side but lower marshy ground on the right bank. There are no villages right on the riverbanks, so this is a peaceful rural walk.

Two lanes lead from the towpath up to Taden village, making a pleasant detour. Until the 11th

century Taden was a port at the tidal limit of the Rance, but its history goes back to Gallo-Roman times. The village developed at a crossroads of both the river and the road between Dinan and St Malo. Aerial photography and subsequent digs have revealed 11 archaeological sites which include two temples. These remains are mainly in the village and on the left bank of the Rance. In the village you can visit the Manoir de la Grand'Cour, a beautifully preserved 14th century manor house.

Dinan

Dinan is an old feudal town with a really impressive location. Perched on top of an almost sheer cliff, far above the river, its ramparts and promenades give absolutely stunning views. Arriving by river you look up towards a huge ten-arch viaduct, 250 metres long and over 40 metres above the towpath. Dinan's quays line the west shore and for centuries were the heart of the city's economic activity. Today the quays are just as busy, but are now lined with private boats, while comfortable *vedettes* offer tourists excursions along the Rance. Along this elegant old waterfront you can find a good choice of restaurants and various boutiques run by local craftsmen.

At the head of the port is a picturesque stone bridge, the lowest bridge on the canal and the one which prevents many boats from using this sheltered route through to the Bay of Biscay. From the end of this bridge, Rue du Petit Fort leads uphill between half-timbered houses to Rue du Jerzual and the upper town. The cobbled medieval streets and 15th century houses are attractive, but they are still lived in and the town has managed to remain a vibrant and working community despite the number of tourists. Galleries and artisans' studios rub shoulders with butchers and bakers, so Dinan town has definitely not become a museum.

Before the viaduct was built, Jerzual Street was the main route into the upper town, and merchants, visitors and local tradesmen all had to toil up it. Place des Merciers has some of the best-preserved half-timbered and decorated houses dating from the 15th century, interspersed with other properties built rather later. Having reached the upper town, don't miss a stroll along the ramparts, a visit to the church of St Malo with its stained glass windows, or a climb to the top of the 15th century clock tower for the amazing views over Dinan and the Rance.

1. A bird's-eye view of Dinan. The ramparts, Petits-Diables garden and the Château Duchesse Anne are all clearly visible.
2 and 3. Many of the half-timbered houses in Dinan date from the 15th century.
4. The quays along the Rance at Dinan.
5. A weaver demonstrating her skill.
6. The old stone bridge across the Rance, just above the port of Dinan.

From Dinard to Cap Fréhel

In the eastern approaches to Cape Fréhel, you pass several strikingly different stretches of coast. Just along from Dinard are the small coves and promontories on the way to St-Briac-sur-Mer, where you reach the Frémur river and the sandy bays of Lancieux and Arguenon with their off-lying islands. On the west side of this wide-sweeping bight is the popular beach and resort of St Cast, sheltered from the west by Pointe de St Cast. Having rounded this headland you arrive at Fresnaye bay where, at low tide, a vast expanse of sand and mud is uncovered, a perfect hunting ground for *la pêche à pied.*

Fort la Latte guards the western edge of Fresnaye and then you can see the stark headland of Cap Fréhel. Standing well out into the Channel, its steep cliffs and treeless heath can look desolate on a grey day, but in high-summer sun this spectacular point is a haze of purple heather and golden gorse.

1. Pointe du Chevet and the Hébihens islands extending away to seaward. The sandbanks that link them at low water are enjoyed by walkers and shellfish gatherers.

1

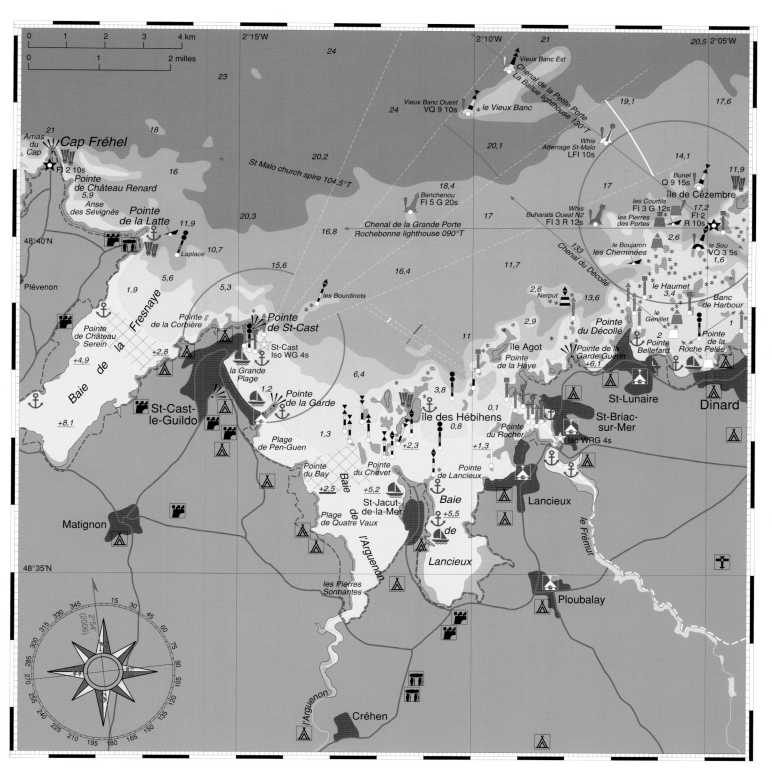

Saint-Lunaire to St Jacut-de-la-Mer

1. Pointe du Décollé and St Lunaire village, with Longchamp beach in the foreground.
2. East of Pointe du Décollé, the sandy beach at St Lunaire is fringed with several large hotels.
3. The anchorage off St Lunaire is sheltered from the prevailing winds by Pointe du Décollé and Petit David rock.

Originally a small fishing village, Saint-Lunaire was transformed into a seaside resort in the mid 19th century. As with Dinard, it became popular with English and American visitors and many wealthy Parisians. The belief that sea-bathing would cure all ills encouraged the upper classes and minor royalty to spend their summers at coastal resorts and many large villas were built at Saint-Lunaire.

The major development of the town started when a very rich Haitian banker, Sylla Laraque, bought a parcel of land close to Pointe du Décollé from a local family (the Ponthuals) which he divided into building plots. A dyke

was built along the beach to protect the area as it was liable to flooding on very high tides. Villas soon appeared, grand hotels along the waterfront, and a casino and tennis courts all attracted more and more visitors. Laraque also had an electricity-generating station built, a bold innovation at the time. The countryside around Saint-Lunaire is very attractive with charming walks out to Pointe de la Garde-Guérin and along the coast.

This area of Brittany, the Emerald Coast, was a popular destination for artists who enjoyed the vibrant colours of the landscape and the wonderful luminescence of the sea. Many stayed at St Briac-sur-Mer, but

today there is little in the town to recall that these enthusiastic painters helped establish its reputation. It is hard to discover any reference to Auguste Renoir, Henri Rivière, Émile Bernard or Paul Signac.

St Briac developed as a fishing harbour at the mouth of the Frémur river. Ships carrying salt from Le Croisic to St Malo, mainly for the Newfoundland cod fishermen, often stopped at La Houle bay as they worked up the coast. As with many small communities in the area, St Briac is really a collection of hamlets that have now grown into a necklace of resorts running along the coast from Dinard. The village is

Saint-Lunaire to St Jacut-de-la-Mer

named after a 6th century Irish saint, whose life story is depicted in the stained glass windows of the 19th century parish church. The bell tower, which is older than the church, is decorated with railings and mouldings which include the arms of the Pontbriand family. Because local fishermen contributed considerable sums to the building of the church, there are carvings of mackerel on the north gable!

Between Pointe de la Garde-Guérin and Pointe de la Haye, an area of land near Port-Hue beach has been bought by the local authority. Under an environmental protection programme, the dunes here have been re-established, and

give spectacular views across to Île Dame-Jouanne close inshore, and Île Agot off the headland. In the approach to St Briac, around Anse de la Houle, you pass a row of bathing huts along the beach. There are lots of boats in the bay, most of which just stay afloat at low tide. Overlooking the beach is the extravagantly decorated Château du Nessay, which is now a summer school for youngsters.

Above the road bridge, the Frémur river flows gently, drying out soon after half-tide. A little way inland you reach the old tide mill of Roche-Good. The river is a favourite place to keep small boats and is also a good hunting ground for

1. Pointe de la Haye and the off-lying island of Agot from the west. In the centre of the photograph is the mouth of the Frémur river and the anchorage at St Briac.
2. Perron island is linked to the mainland by a sandbank off Pointe de la Haye.
3. The mermaid sculpture on the bell tower of the old Lancieux church.
4. Looking towards St Briac from the north-west.
5. The anchorage off Béchet beach is sheltered by the headland but dries at low water.
6. St Sieuc is the main beach at the holiday resort of Lancieux.
7. Beach huts line the edge of Anse de la Houle.

shellfish. Between L'Islet and Pointe du Rocher is a sheltered drying area – it can hardly be called a port, but small boats can find their way in here near the top of the tide.

The sea enters Lancieux bay through a narrow gap between Pointe de Buglais and Pointe St Jacut. With its wide beach, this is a popular place to search for cockles, whelks and other shellfish. The little drying harbour, with its two landing slips, is usually full of small boats.

1		
2	4 5	6
3		7

Saint-Lunaire to St Jacut-de-la-Mer

1. Close to its mouth, a long road bridge crosses the Frémur river. To the left is Lancieux village and beach with Île des Hébihens in the distance.
2. Pointe du Rocher and the off-lying L'Islet enclose the mouth of the Frémur to the west.
3. Horse riding along the edge of the Frémur river at low tide.
4. At the head of the Frémur inlet is Roche-Good tide mill.

5. Lancieux bay is enclosed on the west by the peninsula of St-Jacut-de-la-Mer, and on the east by the meadows at Ploubalay.

The village is up behind St Sieuc beach and you can see the bell tower that was built in 1740 (the church was destroyed in 1904). At the base of the tower is a small carving of a mermaid and the shield of the Glé family. Robert Service, a Canadian poet, often spent summers in Lancieux, at a villa he bought and renamed *Dream Haven*. He died there in 1958 and is buried in the cemetery. Near the road to Ploubalay, the 16th century Buglais mill was built by the monks of St Jacut abbey. It was still working during World War II and was restored by the town in the 1970s.

Tucked into the west side of a narrow peninsula, St-Jacut-de-la-Mer has a distinctive character. The village grew around the abbey founded by a 5th century Welsh monk, Jacut, which later came under the Benedictine order. At that time St Jacut, like Mont St Michel, was an island at high tide. It wasn't until a causeway was built and sand gradually banked up to broaden it that the island was finally connected to the mainland.

The residents of St Jacut, called Jagüens, have retained the characteristics of islanders. For centuries they were cut off from their neighbours, speaking a type of Gallic with something of a Welsh, sing-song accent and a colourful vocabulary. More than half the population continued to speak this patois until after World War II. Jaguins tended to intermarry and were proud, stubborn and often quarrelsome folk. They were formidable fishermen, mostly for mackerel and skate, and frequently competed for catches with fishermen from St Cast and St Briac.

Their boats were six or seven metres long with fine bows and a lugger rig. This sort of boat performed well in strong winds and the short chop encountered in the bays. There is no real port at St Jacut, just drying anchorages at Lancieux, Houle-Causseul and Châtelet. These places are only accessible for a few small boats near the top of the tide.

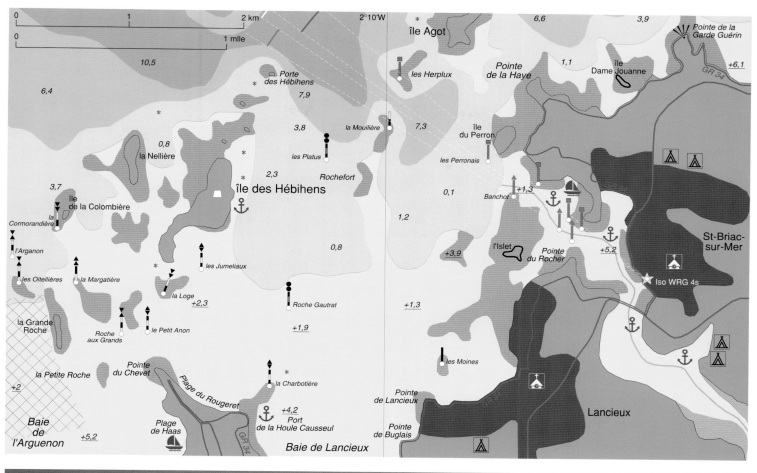

0

1

2 km

0

1 mlle

2°10'W

*

6,6

3,9

Île Agot

*

Pointe de la Garde Guérin

+6,1

10,5

les Herplux

Pointe de la Haye

1,1

Île Dame Jouanne

GR 34

6,4

Porte des Hébihens

*

7,9

0,8

la Mouilière

la Nellière

3,8

7,3

Île du Perron

*

les Platus

les Perronais

2,3

Rochefort

3,7

Île des Hébihens

0,1

Banchot

+1,3

St-Briac-sur-Mer

île de la Colombière

*

1,2

l'Islet

Pointe du Rocher

+5,2

la Cormorandière

0,8

+3,9

l'Arganon

les Jumeliaux

Iso WRG 4s

les Oitellières

la Margatière

*

la Loge

+2,3

Roche Gautrat

+1,3

la Grande Roche

Roche aux Grands

le Petit Anon

+1,9

la Petite Roche

Pointe du Chevet

les Moines

Pointe de Lancieux

+2

Plage du Rougeret

la Charbotière

*

Lancieux

Plage de Haas

+4,2

Port de la Houle Causseul

Pointe de Buglais

Baie de l'Arguenon

+5,2

GR 34

Baie de Lancieux

Île des Hébihens and the sandbanks off Pointe du Chevet.

Les Hébihens and Arguenon bay

1. Île des Hébihens and Lancieux bay seen from the west.
2. The paradise beaches on Île des Hébihens.
3. The islet of Nellière, just north-west of Île des Hébihens, is home to a colony of common terns.
4. Pointe du Chevet. At low water you can walk out to Île des Hébihens.
5. Oyster cultivation in Arguenon bay. The vast stretches of sand that uncover at low water are ideal for mussel and oyster farming. The racks and stakes are tended regularly.

Île des Hébihens is a favourite weekend anchorage for yachts from St Malo. On the east side of the island, in the shelter of Pointe de la Chapelle, boats are protected from the prevailing winds. This bay is a charming place to linger on warm summer days and the clear water over fine sand is enticing for swimming. From St Jacut you can walk to the island on a low spring tide, although Hébihens is private property. A fortified tower was built here in 1696 on the orders of Vauban and Count Louis de Pontbriand, to defend the bays either side of St Jacut peninsula. This project was financed by a tax on the mackerel catch taken on five feast days, that would have been holidays.

Recent archaeological digs have shown evidence of an early Celtic village that includes several dwellings and a workshop for producing blocks of salt. A 13th century bread oven has also been revealed. The diminutive Arguenon river rises close to the Rance in the Côtes d'Armor hills and flows through Plancoët into Arguenon bay, which opens to the sea between Pointe du Chevet and Pointe du Bay. The only obstructions in the bay are the black oyster racks and thin chestnut withies marking them, which vanish in bad weather, bending under the combination of gusts of wind and the waves.

At low water the bay is an expanse of sparkling wet sand, but the movement of tractors back up the beach and the swing of boats near Île des Hébihens and Île de la Colombière hint at the returning tide. The fresh water from the Arguenon river is soon swallowed up by the sea, the flood reaching right to the foot of Plancoët church. The ruins of the 14th century Guildo castle are visible on the right bank of the estuary as you round Pointe de la Pépinais. The original fortress had four towers connected by thick walls, with foundations built into the rock. Henri IV ordered it to be destroyed

Les Hébihens and Arguenon bay

89

and by the late 18th century it was already a ruin.

The small trading port of Le Guildo is mostly kept open by a timber yard, whose wharf is often piled high with logs from Scandinavia. Occasional coasters also deliver Dutch fertilizer to a new wharf built for them in the early 1970s. When walking along its banks it's difficult to believe that the Arguenon is a navigable river. It seems that for too much of the time the sea abandons this channel to sand and mud, and yet good-sized ships once sailed up to Plancoët. There are accounts in old documents of these navigations:

'Plancoët has a port where for three days before and four days after a spring tide, 30 to 40 ton vessels can enter. On equinoctial tides, there are even some that reach 60 and 70 tons. The official registers of the commune bear witness to the launching of ships of large tonnages. But the narrow width between the docks and the sharp curves of the channel require that ships over 18 metres be hauled from the stern.'

There is no easy riverside path to Plancoët, but you can follow the by-road that connects Le Guildo to Créhen and cross the river towards Le Vieux Bourg.

'If I experienced happiness, it was certainly in Plancoët,' wrote Chateaubriand, who lived as a small child with his grandmother in the Nazareth quarter of the town. Chateaubriand was delicate as a young boy and the fresh air and country food were good for

1. Arguenon bay looking towards the sea.
2. Arguenon river with the timber yard in the foreground.
3. A fishing boat dried out in the Arguenon river.

him. Later he spent many summer holidays at his grandmother's house, and also at the Manoir de Monchoix at Pluduno, which belonged to his uncle.

4. The tiny port at Le Guildo.
5. The 16th century Manoir du Val belonged to the poet Hippolyte de la Morvonnais.
6. Quatre-Vaux beach.
7. The Arguenon River at low water.
8. The ruins of Guildo castle on the right bank, downstream of the bridge.
9. Timber at the docks at Le Guildo.

1	2	
3	4	5	6
	7	8	9

St-Cast-le-Guildo

1. The sweeping Grande Plage at St-Cast-le-Guildo, with Pointe de la Garde in the foreground and Pointe de St Cast on its north side. Behind St Cast you can see the edge of Fresnaye bay, with rows of oyster racks.
2. Between Pointe de la Garde and Pointe du Bay is the fine sandy beach of Pen-Guen, one of the seven beaches of St Cast. You can also see the St Cast golf course.

3. The slipway and anchorage at Pointe de la Garde are sheltered by the headland.
4. An air-sea rescue helicopter takes off on a reconnais-sance flight from the semaphore station on Pointe de St Cast.
5. St Cast harbour, where there is now a deepwater marina.

St Cast is another of the charming villages on this coast that developed into a summer resort in the second half of the 19th century. Along with Saint-Lunaire, Dinard and St Briac, it gradually transformed into a desirable location for bathing and seawater cures. With the arrival of a train service from Paris to Lamballe in 1858, a holiday in Brittany became a real possibility for a large proportion of the population.

Alfred Marinier, a painter, was captivated by the charms of St Cast and became its enthusiastic champion. He enjoyed the bays and beaches, the pine trees on the headlands and the colourful boats in the little harbour. He bought the land on and around Pointe de la Garde and built the Hôtel de la Plage, encouraging his friends to come and stay in the hotel and then to build villas and cottages in the area. St Cast rapidly became known as the Peninsula of the Seven Beaches and the attractions of this welcoming family resort encouraged more and more visitors.

Pointe de la Garde, at the south end of La Grande Plage, is a wooded peninsula with secluded residential properties. By following the tourist trail around the point you will arrive at one of the most beautiful views of the Hébihens archipelago. From its vantage well out into the bay, the panorama takes in the coastline all the way from Cap Fréhel to the St Malo approaches and Pointe de la Varde.

With the huge range of tide, acres of sand uncover on Grande Plage at low water. The sea wall protects the promenade, which runs the length of the beach. Around the town you can see many examples of early 20th century seaside villas. At high tide the sea comes right up to the wall and in strong winds breaking waves send spray flying over the promenade.

Paul Sébillot was a late 19th century painter and writer who was

particularly interested in the folklore of Brittany and Normandy. He wrote many books about local legends and fairy stories that brought old tales to the attention of a new audience. One of these stories was about the pixies that lived in the underground cave of La Houle, near St Cast, who notified the human world that they had done a good deed by knocking under the hearth.

The old part of St Cast is clustered around the church. Inside there is a 12th century font decorated with grinning devils, with statues of St Cast and St Clement dating from the 17th century. The present church was built in the 1890s but only consecrated in 1932, the same year the organ was installed.

On 4th September 1758, in the middle of the Seven Years War, a British army force landed at Pointe de la Garde-Guérin to launch an attack on St Malo. The soldiers were commanded by General Bligh, but things didn't go to plan. Bligh decided to rejoin the fleet anchored in the Bay of St Cast. The Duke of Aiguillon was waiting there and a fierce battle ensued with enormous losses on both sides. The Moulin d'Anne was an observation post and headquarters for the Duke of Aiguillon during the conflict. The duke was reputed to be having an affair with the miller's wife and there is now a *pâtisserie* in St Cast named after her, *Belle Meunière*.

The old fishermen's quarter, Le Quartier de l'Isle, is on the way towards Pointe de St Cast. Here, the small cottages have coloured windows and it's fun to explore the narrow alleyways. There is also a small drying harbour for boats owned mostly by recreational fishermen. St Cast has a commercial fishing fleet, though the numbers have been much reduced to about 20 over the last few years. They mostly dredge for scallops in the winter and set pots for fish and lobster for the rest of the year. After much recent planning and discussion, St Cast now has a new deepwater marina.

1. An isolated danger beacon marks Feuillade rock in St Cast harbour.
2. Many boats in St Cast are moored fore and aft to buoys.
3. The old Ar Vro hotel above the Grande Plage at St Cast.
4. The outer breakwater at St Cast harbour.
5. Belle Époque villas and hotels still line the waterfront behind La Grande Plage at St Cast.
6. Youngsters from the sailing school out in Optimists.

1	2
3	4	6
	5	

La Fresnaye Bay

1. La Fresnaye bay with Pointe du Muret on the left. At the edge of the tideline you can just make out the lines of oyster racks and mussel stakes.
2. The little beach of Mare near Pointe de St Cast.
3. La Fresnaye bay, with Pointe du St Efficace sheltering the mouth of Port St Jean creek.

1	
2	3

The long shallow inlet called Baie de la Fresnaye is almost rectangular in shape and cuts into the Brittany mainland for nearly three miles. For most of its length the bay is about a mile wide and virtually all this vast expanse dries out to muddy sand on a good low water. The entrance to Fresnaye lies a couple of miles south-east of Cap Fréhel, just inside Pointe de la Latte, and the mouth of the bay was a strategic and well-used anchorage in the days of sail. Cap Fréhel is a bold and easily identified landfall for vessels approaching from the north, and even for relatively cumbersome ships it would have been a simple matter to alter course a shade to the east and make for the anchorage opposite Pointe de la Cierge.

This anchorage had several advantages apart from being simple to identify and sail into. This was, and still is, a very sheltered spot in strong westerlies and south-westerlies, and most ships could comfortably ride out gales from these quarters. Just as important, the anchorage would also have been easy to leave under sail when the depression was past and the wind had veered to north-westerly before gradually moderating. Leaving Baie de la Fresnaye in a north-westerly would have been a safe and simple reach, and from here the main entrance channel into St Malo – Chenal de la Grande Porte – is only about five miles due east. This approach would have been an easy run for any sailing ship, even heavily laden.

Nowadays this traditional passage anchorage is only visited by a few yachts on warm summer days, and otherwise Fresnaye is one of the most peaceful corners of the Côte d'Émeraude. A wide area just inside the charted drying contour is used for mussel beds, and the cool waters and fast-moving tides provide ideal conditions for growing *moules de la Fresnaye*. At low water at spring tides, the mussel workers can drive right out onto the sands aboard specially designed amphibious mussel barges – half-boat, half-tractor – to tend to the young molluscs.

An evocative description of shellfish cultivation in Brittany appears in the memoirs of Monsieur de Gastines, who writes lyrically

about the art of rearing mussels and oysters in large tidal bays:

'Imagine fields that live to the rhythm of the tides, a world where the cry of seagulls replaces the crow of the cock. Imagine a different type of farmer who abandons the tractor to get about, instead, by boat. Part sailor, part farmer, they have shaped the art of rearing shellfish from generation to generation . . .'

In the south-west corner of La Fresnaye Bay, a tiny traditional harbour, Port Nieux, is protected by Pointe du Muret and a single stone jetty from almost any kind of weather. Although Port Nieux is only accessible by boat for less than two hours each side of a good high tide, this small haven was once used by sailing coasters and barges

for loading grain from the nearby farming villages of Pléhérel, Plévenon, Pléboulle and Matignon.

The jetty at Port Nieux was built in the mid 19th century, and by the 1870s this now seemingly remote harbour handled about 130 ships of between 70 and 150 tons, as well as nearly 100 smaller coasters that brought in bulk cargoes such as timber, iron, coal and limestone. These vessels would arrive right at the top of a high tide and then sit safely on the sandy bottom of the harbour as the ebb ran away. There are many forgotten harbours like this all around the Brittany coast.

On the south-east side of the Bay, at the head of a narrow drying creek behind Pointe St Efficace, an old tidal mill can still be seen near the hamlet of St Germain. The

simple but highly effective mills – *moulins à marée* – were important all along the Côte d'Émeraude, where the massive tides provided a reliable free source of renewable energy.

La Fresnaye Bay

93

1. The receding tide creates artistic patterns and ripples in the mud of La Fresnaye bay.
2. On the north-west shore, well into the bay, you'll find the tiny drying harbour and quay at Porte Nieux.
3. A rural scene on the banks of the Frémur.
4. The shoreline under Pointe de Crissouet supports a fascinating range of wildlife.
5. The anchorage and landing slip at Port St Géran.
6. Old rotting hulls at Porte Nieux.

1	2	
3	4 / 5	6

Fort la Latte

1. Fort la Latte is built on a rocky outcrop. You can clearly see the two faults that separate it from the coast and the two drawbridges needed to reach it. From the top of the tower and the walkway, there are exceptional views out to sea and along the coast. The anchorage in the lee of the point, just south-east of the fort, is popular on summer days.

1

Not far along the coast west of St Cast, Cap Fréhel is an unmistakable headland, topped by its powerful lighthouse. Less than two miles to the east, on a slightly lower point, stands an imposing and rather ornate castle, Fort la Latte. The castle is perched right on the end of the jutting finger of Pointe de la Latte, with commanding sea views.

This sturdy medieval fortress was the home of the Goyon-Matignon family during the 13th and 14th centuries. Its naturally defensive position on the headland, with two crevasses crossed by drawbridges on the landward side, made Fort la Latte virtually impregnable through-out numerous wars. At the end of the 16th century, during the Wars of Religion, the fort was severely burnt, so when Vauban inspected it

most of the defences were in ruins. His trusty engineer, Siméon de Garangeau, was responsible for rebuilding the fort, much as we see it today. In 1715 the Scottish 'Old Pretender', James Stuart, used La Latte as a base when he was gathering his forces before trying to take the English throne. In World War II, the Germans used the fort as a lookout and defensive position.

In more recent, less warlike times, several films have been located there, probably the most famous being *The Vikings*, directed by Richard Fleischer. The cast included Kirk Douglas and Tony Curtis, so you can picture the extravagant scenes around the ramparts and drawbridges.

The fort was constructed as a rectangle with enormously strong

towers around its walls, 60 metres above the sea, and a traditional keep in the centre. An interesting 18th century addition was a furnace where cannonballs could be heated until they were red-hot. When one of these hit a wooden sailing ship it would inevitably catch fire.

Although it is privately owned the fort is open to visitors from Easter to September and a climb up the 15th century lookout tower is included in the tour. Just outside the castle stands a rather enigmatic looking megalith, said to be either the finger of the giant Gargantua or else a mark for the place where his head rests in its tomb. A largish chap, his feet are apparently 25 kilometres away at St Suliac.

The impressive headland of Cap Fréhel defines the eastern extremity of Baie de St Brieuc and juts more than two kilometres into the Channel. From the Fresnaye anchorage under Pointe de la Cierge, it's about three miles by boat to reach Cap Fréhel and turn this dramatic corner towards Baie de St Brieuc. From seaward, the fort on Pointe de la Latte looks very striking, with a cylindrical keep inside the elegant but determined-looking walls that take up most of the promontory.

A quarter of a mile north of Pointe de la Latte lurks a notorious rocky shoal, which is only just covered at low-water springs. Yachts and fishing boats always give this point a wide berth when coming out of Fresnaye. Another potentially dangerous shoal straggles east of Cap Fréhel, a long rocky spur which is safely covered at high water but whose west end peeks above the surface on a spring low tide.

Cap Fréhel is a dramatic headland, its sheer straight edge looming high above the sea and the north-facing cliffs usually rather dark and dour except early on a summer morning or in the rich westerly light of late afternoon. The ornate square lighthouse stands back from the cliffs, its light 85 metres above sea level.

Half a mile due west of Cap Fréhel is a steep rocky islet called Amas du Cap, a spectacular granite wedge looking like an enormous shark's fin. Like many prominent rocks off the Breton coast, Amas du Cap forms part of a useful leading line for mariners, a transit which leads through safe water with dangers either side. For boats heading west towards the Erquy channel, keeping Amas du Cap just touching the north edge of Fréhel and bearing 077° true astern, leads safely WSW for four miles to where a new set of leading marks takes over. This visual trick of navigating through tricky gaps has been used by seafarers since time immemorial.

Cap Fréhel and the heathland behind it are part of the commune of Plévenon, but this promontory feels wild and remote as the nearest habitation is a long way inland. Although the soil here is thin and poor, the carpet of broom, gorse and heather creates a subtle pattern of colours throughout the seasons. At the extreme edge of the headland, the cliffs drop almost vertically

1. Cap Fréhel seen from the south-east. The high cliffs of shale and red sandstone are dotted with patches of yellow gorse from early in the spring. During the summer, the headland turns pink with heather before becoming purple and bronze in autumn. It's hardly surprising that so many painters were fascinated by Fréhel's many moods.

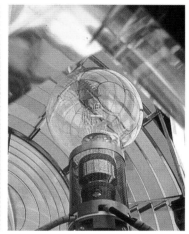

Cap Fréhel

1. Cap Fréhel lighthouse is one of the most powerful on the north coast of Brittany. The light is 85 metres above sea level, has a range of 29 miles and flashes twice every ten seconds. In poor visibility a foghorn sounds twice every minute.
2. The earlier lighthouse dates from the reign of Louis XIV. Initially a coal fire was lit, but was later replaced with a fish-oil burner. The present structure was built in 1950 to replace the lighthouse destroyed by the Germans during World War II.
3. The Vauban tower is perfectly preserved, built of Chausey granite and designed by Siméon de Garangeau.
4. The actual bulb and Fresnel lens at the top of the lighthouse.

to the sea, with rocky chunks at the bottom which appear to have dropped off over the centuries. On wild days, waves seem to explode at the base of the point, throwing up great clouds of spray.

Inevitably, with a location that feels as mysterious as this, legends have been passed down through the generations. One explanation for the pink colour of the cliffs at Cap Fréhel relates to an Irish saint who had come over to Brittany to convert the population. After he had been preaching to a crowd of people, the local baron challenged him thus: 'St Michel was a messenger from God, and when he stepped on the Mont it turned red. You say you are also sent by God, so can you make the cliffs red?' Not long afterwards, the saint walked to Cap Fréhel, cut his finger and a drop of blood fell onto the ground. Immediately all the cliffs were coloured red.

From Fort la Latte, you can reach the headland by the coast path passing above Anse de Sévigné. At the north edge of the bay is the Château Renard promontory, from where you might see overfalls on the Étendrée bank. From the footpath you have wonderful opportunities to see some of the birds that nest in the area and colonize the off-lying rocks.

The cliffs around Cap Fréhel are classified as a nature reserve. The steep inaccessible coast and the many rocks and islets just offshore all create an ideal habitat for a great range of seabirds. The two islets of Grande and Petite Fauconnière support colonies of guillemots and razorbills. Here you may also see oystercatchers, gannets and kittiwakes nesting in the cliffs. On the west side of the headland you might also spot petrels at Pointe du Jas. The craggy islet known as Amas du Cap is protected as a bird sanctuary and is

home to a very rare species on this coast, the common raven. With its striking black plumage, massive beak, long pointed wings and characteristic croak, this rather forbidding bird is easy to identify. In flight it looks like a large bird of prey, but ravens are also scavengers, picking up dead animals or plants. Their courtship display is spectacular, a form of aerial acrobatics. Ravens usually nest on the cliff or inland in old quarries.

Cap Fréhel lighthouse stands back from the cliff edge and its beam has a range of 29 nautical miles. The present lighthouse was built in 1950 to replace the 1847 light which was destroyed by the Germans during the last war. Closer to the cliff edge is the old lighthouse, known as the Vauban

tower, built in 1695 to the plans of the engineer Siméon de Garangeau. The light originally came from a coal fire lit at the top of the tower, but later fish oil was burned. Today, as with almost all lighthouses, Cap Fréhel is completely automatic.

Turning inland you cross 400 hectares of moorland, one of the largest such areas in France. On an overcast day or in the winter, this might appear a bleak and uninteresting landscape, but these moors create rare and delicate habitats. Mainly made up of gorse, heather and broom, other plants can be found during the seasons, such as wild thyme, sea pink and hyacinths. Covering the thinnest soils and rocks you'll find dozens of mosses and lichens. As the sun returns and summer follows spring,

the moorland explodes into scents and colours, humming with insects and wildlife.

1. Cap Fréhel seen from the west. In the foreground is the prominent islet, Amas du Cap.

2, 3 and 4. In the first warm days of spring, the gorse, broom and heather start to flower. The large number of visitors every year are starting to cause concern because of soil erosion and damage to the vegetation.
5. The strange fault line called La Banche opens up on the side of Pointe du Jas.

KENTISH PLOVER
Vulnerable to disturbance, it is perfectly camouflaged to nest in the sand.

BLACKHEADED GULL
Huge flocks of Blackheaded Gull are present from the end of June to the end of March; they nest in fresh water, not on the coast.

DUNLIN
Easily recognized by their plumage, characteristic behaviour and distinctive cry, they are adept at fishing.

CURLEW
A ubiquitous inhabitant of the shoreline, its evocative call is part of the sounds of the coast.

RAY EGGS
It's actually the empty thorny capsule that protects the immature fish.

1. LUGWORM, 2. RAGWORM, 3. SAND HOPPER
These invertebrates are found in different areas of the shore.

PEREGRINE FALCON
These winter visitors are attracted by the vast numbers of birds.

BRENT GOOSE
Small protected species of geese, they graze in flocks of thousands. An impressive spectacle when they head to their night time roost.

Wildlife habitats

98

More than 100 million cubic metres of water enters and leaves the bay on each tide, depositing a million cubic metres of sediment annually. As the ebb is less powerful than the flood this means the bay is steadily silting up, by an average 3mm a year.

The mud and silt brought in by the tide are trapped by plants, worms and other creatures that live in it. The finer sediments are carried further into the bay, close to the long foreshore, and make up what was called *tangue*. This used to be gathered in large quantities and used by local farmers and peasants as fertilizer.

Mudflats are a difficult environment to inhabit and few species can tolerate the changes in salinity and the low oxygen levels: ragworm and small crustaceans are the only species that colonize the area in significant numbers. Fish and cuttlefish return to the bay with the incoming tide, though some remain over low water in the tidal channels. Up on the beaches and the neighbouring saltmarshes, debris brought in by the tide builds up providing a unique home to some highly specialized plants such as the sea rocket or invertebrates such as sand-hoppers. It is here that the Kentish plover nests and large numbers of waders and migratory birds come to feed. This is a very fragile environment, easily damaged by gales or pollution.

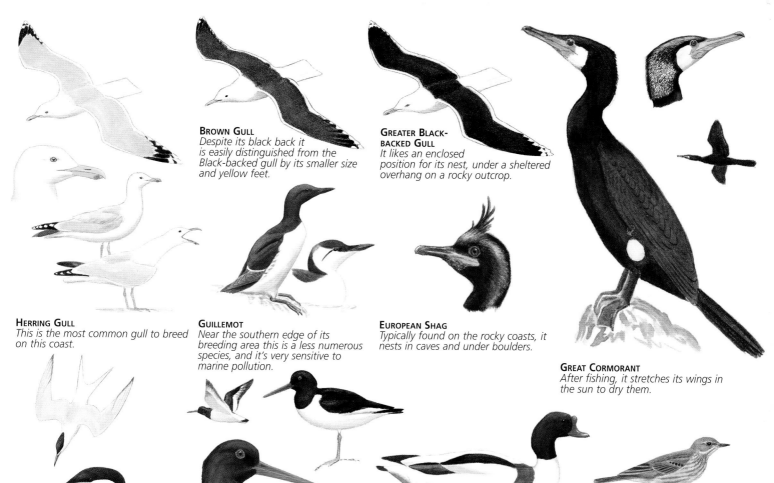

BROWN GULL
Despite its black back it is easily distinguished from the Black-backed gull by its smaller size and yellow feet.

GREATER BLACK-BACKED GULL
It likes an enclosed position for its nest, under a sheltered overhang on a rocky outcrop.

HERRING GULL
This is the most common gull to breed on this coast.

GUILLEMOT
Near the southern edge of its breeding area this is a less numerous species, and it's very sensitive to marine pollution.

EUROPEAN SHAG
Typically found on the rocky coasts, it nests in caves and under boulders.

GREAT CORMORANT
After fishing, it stretches its wings in the sun to dry them.

COMMON TERN
Less robust than gulls, they nest in colonies to make it easier to defend their territories.

OYSTERCATCHER
A shoreline bird, male and female look identical. A cry of alarm indicates its nest is nearby.

COMMON SHELDUCK
It nests in cavities and rabbit holes and feeds mostly on marine invertebrates.

ROCK PIPIT
A stocky little bird, usually seen hopping around rocky shorelines.

There are three main categories of birds that breed along this coastline. First are the truly pelagic species which spend their lives on the high seas, only coming ashore to breed; this includes the northern fulmar and black-legged kittiwake. The breeding season is an ideal time to observe them at close quarters.

Next are the shoreline birds that feed near the coast, the diving seabirds such as the common guillemot, shag, cormorants, gulls, terns, some waders and ducks.

Then there are the terrestrial species that enjoy the favourable conditions and environments on the mainland, for example ravens, finches or starlings. Some sites bring together several of the species which can be seen between April and July.

The bird sanctuary at Cap Fréhel occupies a landscape of cliffs and moorland. It attracts large colonies of shag, black-legged kittiwake and sea gulls. It is the only nesting site for diving seabirds on this part of the coast, with the fulmar at the western extremity of its breeding range.

Separated from the mainland by a powerful current, Landes Island offers a peaceful breeding site that attracts large cormorants and shelducks. Some species nest in smaller and more isolated groups along the shoreline where the conditions are favourable. Possibly the rarest of these are the Kentish plover and the little ringed plover.

Nesting birds

LOBSTER
Renowned but now quite rare, it's still found in rock crevasses on the seabed.

OYSTER AND MUSSEL
These filter feeders are very sensitive to water quality. They can still occasionally be gathered wild from natural banks.

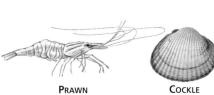

PRAWN

There are many different species occupying different locations; cockles like silt, clams need coarse sand and

COCKLE

SURF CLAM

CLAM

prawns are found in rocky areas. They each need a different fishing technique.

WINKLE
Very common along the shoreline, they are also essential to a plateau de fruits de mer.

ORMER
A very rare species, it is also called a sea-ear because of the shape of its shell.

VELVET SWIMMING CRAB
Its blue/black shell is quite bristly. It can grow to 18 inches and has delicate meat.

WRACK
There are several species of this seaweed which is important to support other flora and fauna.

LIMPET
Sometimes called Chinese hats, once under water, limpets move slowly across the rocks to feed.

The rocky foreshore

The rocky foreshore is a wonderful habitat with a multitude of species, each marvellously adapted to its own niche. You'll find red, green and brown seaweeds, possibly being grazed by limpets and winkles, there will be mussels and sponges, predators such as sea snails and scavengers like sea urchins or dog whelks. Kelp and seaweed were traditionally used to produce soda for the glass industry or iodine, but in the 21st century they are constituents of foodstuffs and cosmetics. Maerl, a mixture of species of red algae, was used for centuries as a soil conditioner and it is now a favourite with organic gardeners.

La pêche à pied is a favourite French pastime, particularly around the Cotentin and Brittany, and at low water dozens of people will be seen poking in the rocks and scraping in the sand. The tools used are many and varied; shrimp nets for rock pools or long hooks to lift then neatly replace the flat stones where crabs hide. A *fouëne* is a special multi-pronged fork with little hooks along the tines to catch eels, while winkles will be harvested in large quantities and mussels can be picked off flat rocks. Clams will be found in the sand using a rake or even a kitchen fork.

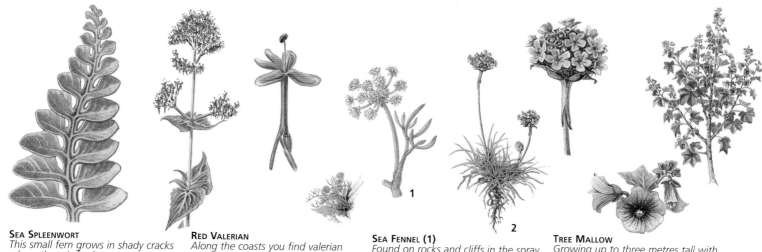

SEA SPLEENWORT
This small fern grows in shady cracks where there is fresh water.

RED VALERIAN
Along the coasts you find valerian with red, pink or white flowers.

SEA FENNEL (1)
Found on rocks and cliffs in the spray, the flowers are typical umbellifers.

SEA PINK (2)
Also known as thrift, this little plant flowers for several months.

TREE MALLOW
Growing up to three metres tall with woolly leaves and purple flowers, tree mallows are easy to identify.

COMMON GORSE
This varies from Western gorse (Ulex gallii) by flowering predominantly in spring.

KESTREL
Often seen hovering over cliffs searching for rodents or insects.

LINNET (3)
Often seen flying in small flocks.

DARTFORD WARBLER (4)
This very shy little bird is most easily identified by its unique song.

COMMON RAVEN
Only a few pairs of these large birds are resident along this rocky coast.

Cliffs and coastal moorlands

The southern coast of the Gulf of St Malo is diverse and varied. There are steep cliffs and headlands, sandy beaches and ranges of dunes, estuaries, inlets and wide bays. The geology is also mixed with red sandstone of Cap Fréhel or mica schist of Pointe du Grouin.

Thousands of people walk the cliff paths every year; Cap Fréhel has over 500,000 visitors. The beautiful landscapes attract all these people but their very numbers cause soil erosion and change the local vegetation. Visitors need to respect these fragile habitats if they are not to be damaged. The original vegetation of coastal moorlands grows on thin soils and is easily eroded by salt laden, gale force winds. You often see stunted trees and shrubs grown into incredible shapes by the prevailing winds, while some species develop prostrate forms to adapt to the conditions.

The moorland changes colour with the seasons, from bright yellow gorse and the white flowers of blackthorn in the spring, followed by the pink heather and wild lilac in early summer, into the purples and bronze tints of autumn.

Kestrels can be seen hovering over the moorland or the cliff edge and the little linnet finds shelter in the heather. It is wonderful to watch the spectacular flight of a raven, which nests in the most inaccessible places as early as February.

Index of places